Wakefield Then & Now

To Caroline, my wife, for all her love, affection, and tireless assistance with this book.
Such a modest soul could never know how delightful she is.

Wakefield Then & Now

Extraordinary Tales from the Merrie City

Michael J. Rochford

PEN & SWORD
HISTORY

First published in Great Britain in 2016 by
Pen & Sword History
an imprint of
Pen & Sword Books Ltd
47 Church Street
Barnsley
South Yorkshire
S70 2AS

ISBN 978 1 47385 848 0

A CIP catalogue record for this book is available from the British Library

Typeset in Ehrhardt by
Mac Style Ltd, Bridlington, East Yorkshire
Printed and bound in the UK by CPI Group (UK) Ltd,
Croydon, CRO 4YY

Pen & Sword Books Ltd incorporates the imprints of Pen & Sword Archaeology, Atlas,
Aviation, Battleground, Discovery, Family History, History, Maritime, Military, Naval, Politics,
Railways, Select, Transport, True Crime, Fiction, Frontline Books, Leo Cooper, Praetorian
Press, Seaforth Publishing and Wharncliffe.

For a complete list of Pen & Sword titles please contact
PEN & SWORD BOOKS LIMITED
47 Church Street, Barnsley, South Yorkshire, S70 2AS, England
E-mail: enquiries@pen-and-sword.co.uk
Website: www.pen-and-sword.co.uk

Contents

Acknowledgements

Thanks go to Pen & Sword, my publisher, for giving me the opportunity to write this book. To Kirsty McHugh, late of the Yorkshire Archaeological and Historical Society, for her kind permission to reproduce images from John W. Walker's collection, and thanks also to Old Maps.co.uk for allowing me to reproduce Ordnance Survey maps of the nineteenth century. Also to Richard Knowles of Rickaro Books for sourcing such scarce Wakefield titles for me. And to Linne Matthews, a most encouraging, supportive and diligent editor.

Kirkgate Station, drawn by Henry Clarke, who was surgeon at Wakefield Prison from 1876 to 1908. The image, believed to have been drawn in the 1890s, shows the station building, which was completed in 1857. *By courtesy of Wakefield Local Studies Library (WLSL).*

Introduction

Just after 11.00 am on Wednesday, 25 August 1869, a train from Huddersfield pulled into the busy Kirkgate Station at Wakefield, smoke billowing from its chimney. It was met by Dr Holdsworth, mayor of the town, accompanied by a number of Wakefield gentlemen. They were assembled to greet Fairless Barber, Esq., secretary of the Huddersfield Archaeological and Topographical Society (which was soon to be renamed the Yorkshire Archaeological Society) who'd brought its members, and a large number of their wives and friends, on a special excursion to Wakefield. The visitors were about to embark on a grand tour of the town and its surroundings, breaking for a fine luncheon at the Great Bull Hotel at the top of Westgate.

The topographers were well aware of the rich history awaiting them in a town that had become a merchant powerhouse of the north by the nineteenth century. It had benefited from the Industrial Revolution and was built on the trades of wool, cloth and grain, possessing thriving markets and a fine array of civic and religious buildings. Its merchant princes, who'd made their fortunes from the success of the town's commerce, lived in palatial mansions in Wakefield and its local townships and villages, their impressive carriages lining Westgate on certain evenings while they gathered at the theatre following days at the races.

A report on the excursion appeared in the local newspaper, the *Wakefield Express*, which read: 'There are few towns in the West Riding, and we might add even in the broad county of York itself, that can boast so rich a store of important historical associations [than] the good old Saxon town of merry Wakefield.' The account went on to describe the schedule for the tour, starting with the noble, spired parish church 'within whose time-worn walls are woven so many interesting traditions of the past,' followed by a visit to the ancient bridge and Chantry Chapel, with the report noting the 'bloody fray' that took place there. This was a reference to the Battle of Wakefield in 1460. The visitors would also take in the Six Chimneys, Heath Old Hall, Sandal Castle and other relics 'around which our fancies play, weaving strange pictures of bygone days.' But it wasn't only Wakefield's buildings that attracted the society, for special notice was paid to its 'thriving townsfolk' who 'proved such gleesome company as to earn for it the cheerful cognomen of Merrie Wakefield.'

The society members weren't the first topographers to visit the town, which appeared as Wachefeld in the Domesday Book and was once famed for its mystery plays. John Leland, the antiquary who'd been chaplain to King Henry VIII, embarked in 1538 on summer journeys throughout England and Wales, describing his observations of the locations he toured in notebooks, collectively known as his itinerary. The following is his account of what he found at Wakefield:

Wakefield upon Calder ys a very quick market-towne and meately large; well served of flesch and fische, both from the se and by rivers, whereof divers be thereabout at hande, so that al vitaile is very gode chepe there. A right honest man shal fare well for two pens a meale. In this towne is but one chefe chirche … There is also a chapel of our Ladye on Calder bridge … A quarter of a mile without Wakefeld apperith an hille of erthe cast up, wher sum say that one of Erles Warines began to build, and as faste as he builded violence of winde defaced the work. This is like a fable. Sum say that it was nothing but a wind mille hill. The place is now called Lohill. The faire bridge of stone of nine arches under the which rennith the river of Calder; and on the est side of this bridge, is a right goodly chapel of our Ladye … Al the hole profite of the toune stondith by course drapery. There be few townes yn the inwarde partes of Yorkshire that hath a fairer site or soile about it. There be plente of veines of se cole in the quarters about Wakefeld.

As well as commenting on the town's industries, the parish church and Chantry Chapel, Leland had noted the apparent site of a castle at Lowe or Lawe Hill, located within what is now Thornes Park. It was believed to have been begun and then abandoned by one of the Warenne family (Earls of Surrey), who'd been granted the manor of Wakefield and estates at Sandal, where the second earl built Sandal Castle, originally from timber. The fabled castle at Lowe Hill is of continuing interest to the modern archaeologist. Indeed, it was announced in 2015 that the site was to be surveyed, with ambitious plans to excavate, sixty years after searches in the 1950s uncovered no hint of any stonework.

Later in the sixteenth century, antiquarian and topographer William Camden followed in Leland's footsteps, and described what he'd seen at Wakefield in his opus *Britannia*. He wrote of a 'towne famous for clothing, for greatnesse, for faire building, a well frequented mercate, and a bridge, upon which King Edward the Fourth erected a beautifull chappell in memoriall of those that lost their lives there in battaile'.

On 30 December 1460, Edward's father, Richard, Duke of York, was killed in the Battle of Wakefield, and Edmund, Earl of Rutland, Edward's brother, was murdered on or about Wakefield Bridge as he fled the battle, as portrayed in William's Shakespeare's *King Henry VI Part 3*. This led the unwitting to assume that the ancient chapel had been built in memory of those who'd fallen. Eighteenth-century prints (and modern reprints) of *A Perspective View of the Chapell Adjoining to Wakefield Bridge*, painted by George Fleming and engraved by William Henry Toms in 1743, also recorded that the chapel was built by King Edward IV in memory of his father and other nobles and gentry slain in the battle. But this assertion was wide of the mark. The Chantry Chapel predates the battle by over a century and was in fact built in stone in the 1300s, between 1342 and 1356. It was on 13 May 1356 when, in return for the sum of twenty marks, King Edward III granted a licence in mortmain vesting the property in the hands of two Wakefield chaplains named William Kay and William Bull.

Seventeenth-century historian and clergyman Dr Thomas Fuller, author of *History of the Worthies of England*, published posthumously, had wondered how the town came upon its nickname, Merrie

Wakefield (or Merry, as he spelt it). He thought it wise not to dwell too deeply: 'What peculiar cause of mirth this town has above others I do not know, and dare not too curiously inquire, lest I turn their mirth among themselves into anger against me.'

Daniel Defoe, author of *Robinson Crusoe* and *Moll Flanders*, visited the town in the eighteenth century, noting in one of his many letters, published in *Curious and Diverting Journies thro' the whole Island of Great Britain* in 1734, that Wakefield was a 'a large, handsome, rich clothing town, full of people, and full of trade'. He also spoke of the battle and the chantry, repeating the erroneous assertion about its founder. Defoe described being shown ground where, until it was removed by Cromwell's troops, once stood 'a large stone cross, in memory of that fatal battle; just upon that spot, the Duke of York fighting desperately, and refusing to yield, tho' surrounded with enemies, was kill'd.' He continued:

> Wakefield is a clean, large, well-built town, very populous and very rich; here is a very large church, and well filled it is, for here are very few Dissenters; the steeple is a very fine spire, and by far the highest in all this part of the country … They tell us, there are here more people also than in the city of York, and yet it is no Corporation town; and the highest magistrate, as I understand, was a constable.
>
> Here also is a market every Friday for woollen cloaths, after the manner of that at Leeds, tho' not so great; yet as all the cloathing trade is encreasing in this country, so this market too flourishes with the rest; not but that sometimes, as foreign markets receive interruption either by wars, by a glut of the goods, or by any other incident, there are interruptions of the manufacture too, which, when it happen, the clothiers are sure to complain of loss of trade; but when the demand comes again they are not equally forward with their acknowledgments; and this, I observed, was the case every where else, as well as here.

Trade directories, or gazetteers, became popular during the nineteenth century and copies of these survive as a useful tool for genealogists and local historians. One of the best to cover Yorkshire was issued by Edward Baines in 1822 as a *History, Directory & Gazetteer of the County of York* in two volumes. Baines said that Wakefield was:

> a large and opulent town delightfully situated, on the left bank of the Calder … The streets are, for the most part, regular, handsome, and spacious, and the houses which are principally of brick, are well built, large, and lofty. In the centre of the market, there is a small, but elegant cross of the Doric order of architecture, with an open colonnade supporting a dome, with an ascent by an open staircase to a spacious room, which is lighted by a lantern, in the dome, and in which room the commissioners of the streets hold their meetings, and other public business is transacted …
>
> The public edifices in Wakefield may be distinguished as ancient and modern. The ancient buildings, are the Parish Church, the Chantry on the bridge, the Free Grammar School, the Charity School, and Haselden Hall; those of more modern date, are, St John's Church, the

Dissenters and Methodist Meeting Houses, the Court House, the Register Office for the West Riding, the Clerk of the Peace's Office, the House of Correction, the West Riding Paper Lunatic Asylum, the Theatre, the Tammy-Hall, the Corn Exchange, and the Public Rooms. The Parish church which is dedicated to All-Saints, is a spacious and lofty Gothic structure, and may be ranked amongst the best Parish churches in the North of England.

In 1871, not long before he died, William Stott Banks, local lawyer and keen topographer and historian, compiled *Walks in Yorkshire: Wakefield and its neighbourhood*. This fine publication was available in two editions, one containing fifty-five woodcuts and the other, a rarity, was further illustrated by photographs of the district, produced by G. & J. Hall, Wakefield photographers, based at 26 Westgate. These images (some of which appear in this book, having been drawn from the collections of the Yorkshire Archaeological and Historical Society), along with Banks's considered and informative text, offered the Victorian tourist visiting Wakefield ample information and illustration to educate and enlighten them as they followed the walks described therein.

In the first decade of the 1900s, the Wakefield City's Tradesmen's Association published a guide to Wakefield, which described the 'City of Today'. It spoke of governance by a mayor, nine aldermen and twenty-seven councillors. It seemed that the city had gained notoriety for its sanitation and its sewage works, which the guide claimed 'is so excellent as to form a model of its kind. Deputations have come from various parts of the world to view these works.' Special praise was reserved for the 'magnificent service of trams … Cars run from the centre of the city into the centre of Leeds, and also into the centre of the neighbouring town of Ossett, the other extremities of the routes being Sandal and Agbrigg.' And by now Wakefield had become the administrative centre of the West Riding of Yorkshire. It operated Petty and Quarter Sessions Courts, a County Court and a Probate Registry. The guide also spoke of Wakefield's two stations, Kirkgate and Westgate, and 'excellent water communication by the Aire and Calder Navigation Co., to Goole, Grimsby, Hull etc.'

In the years that followed, the local corporation issued handbooks promoting the city. One of which, published in the 1950s, gave the following account:

Although Wakefield is a city strongly industrial in character, it also possesses the air of a country town and there are many pleasant walks in the vicinity.

A walk through the city will reward the sightseer with a view of many fine buildings both ancient and modern.

The Corporation have encouraged and assisted development in the centre of the city and Wakefield now has in the Bull Ring, Northgate and Kirkgate, a modern shopping centre which is unequalled by any other town of similar size!

But how has the city and its surroundings changed in the years since Baines, Banks and writers of the twentieth century, and those who came before them? And what stories of old Wakefield might be told anew to the modern reader?

The following pages, illustrated by contemporary and modern photographs (the latter taken by Caroline Rochford), and drawings by Kilby, Clarke, Fennell and others, do not attempt to tell the history of Wakefield; first published as a single volume in 1934, J.W. Walker's *Wakefield its History and People* remains the standard work. In each chapter, glimpses of the past are taken and tales are told through eyewitness accounts, old books, contemporary sources, and newspaper reports of events that occurred in this proud town, lately a city and metropolitan district.

With the parish church as the starting and finishing point, this book follows the layout of the main medieval thoroughfares of Northgate, Kirkgate, Warrengate and Westgate. Some of the accounts, and especially so in the final chapter, allow for a departure to some of the villages outside the city, but the book's essential focus is old Wakefield, with comparable images of then and now included alongside the narrative.

These are the tales of the people and landmarks that have made Wakefield not only a merry city, but an extraordinary one.

Michael J. Rochford
Wakefield, 2016

Chapter One

The Parish Church of All Saints, lately Wakefield Cathedral

Facing the west door, visitors to Wakefield Cathedral can't help but feel a sense of awe at the sheer height of the spire, rising from the great tower and standing at a total of 247 feet tall, before they enter the church and behold an eclectic mix of ancient architecture and modern interior design. Victorian stalls and pews have come and gone, the nave now served by removable seating to allow multiuse of the space, for it isn't only religious worship that takes place in this building, which dates back many centuries, but fairs, exhibitions and concerts, too. The site is Saxon, though the church Norman, with a surviving wall dating back to about 1150. The church was rebuilt in 1329 and improved in 1469. It has been refreshed and renewed several times over the years, notably in 1904, when the chancel, transept, a new crypt and St Mark's Chapel were erected in a new east end extension, and not least in the current era, the nave being restored in 2012 and 2013, and major work on the quire completed in May 2016.

Many years ago, long before the 1904 extension, eighteenth-century veteran church sexton Peter Priestley lived in a little house close to the churchyard. He occupied it with his wife, Lidia, née Bradley, whom he'd married at the parish church on 23 November 1757. Priestley was a solemn man, taking his work very seriously. On Sundays he could be heard leading the congregation in their responses, calling out 'amen' a fraction of a second before everyone else followed suit. He was also responsible for cutting the letters of the names of Wakefield's dearly departed into the stones destined to mark their graves until eternity, or at least until the grim Yorkshire weather bore them illegible. One night, which the *Yorkshire Evening Post* edition of 4 February 1925 reckoned was a Saturday about the year 1791, Peter had grave business to attend to on the ground floor of the church tower. There are several versions of this story, but a fact they all have in common is that Peter was wearing a bob-wig, the sort that is grey with a short ponytail and curls at either sides by the ears. In the first volume of his *Yorkshire Oddities*, author Sabine Baring-Gould, of *Onward Christian Soldiers* fame, informed his readers that the wig was the gift of Revered Michael Bacon, Doctor of Divinity, Vicar of Wakefield. Baring-Gould claimed that Reverend Bacon was prone to bouts of ire when he didn't get his own way, and that this irritation would, on occasion, lead to the clergyman knocking his wig with his right hand in a temper, which in turn led to the gifted wig being rather misshapen by the time it came into the hands of the sexton. That night in 1791, when Peter set off to walk the short distance to the church, Lidia, as she always did, stopped her husband, straightened his wig, and wished him a safe return.

Gould insisted that the night in question was St Mark's Eve, which falls on 24 April each year, a Sunday in 1791. It was said that upon the striking of midnight, apparitions of the souls destined

All Saints Church Wakefield, 1824, drawn by C. Mountain, engraved by T. Higham.

An interior view of All Saints Church Wakefield, 1824, by J.C. Buckler and T. Higham.

to die that year would appear in churches on the eve of St Mark's Day, each in possession of a corpse candle, led on an ethereal procession by a phantom priest, calling, in a softly tone, the words of the burial service. Other accounts of Peter's story say it took place on a cold, moonless winter's night.

Anyway, alone in the tower, with only the light of a single candle, Peter chipped away at his work, occasionally glancing through the doors into the darkness of the nave, discerning no sound, and returning to the job in hand as he whistled the tune of a psalm or two to pass the time. His task was a tedious one, but he could afford no mistakes, so he went about it slowly, accompanied by the chimes of the ninth, tenth and eleventh hours, each marked by the bell in the clock tower. As midnight approached, the waning wax of his candle limiting the time that remained before total darkness rendered his occupation useless, Peter thought about going home, but he just had a few more letters to carve. He brought the candle closer so he

Wakefield Cathedral interior in 2015, following extensive restoration to the nave and the removal of fixed seating.

could check his work in the fading light. It was then that the tones of midnight rang out, and when they subsided Peter heard a frightful hissing. Agitated by this sudden, strange noise, he looked about him but could not discern the source. It grew louder, an unnatural sound that seemed to be accompanied by a most unexpected, and not altogether pleasant, smell. Was this a sign from the Almighty? A warning not to break the Sabbath? Had some ghost been sent to drag him to his end? Down went hammer and chisel, the clatter echoing through the church as Peter snuffed out his candle and beat a hasty retreat. So familiar was he with the interior of the parish church, he almost floated through the nave and out of the west door without disturbing a single hymnal, before turning the handle to his front door and collapsing into his favourite chair.

Lidia had waited up, knowing her husband would welcome a warm drink on his return. Upon seeing his ashen face, she couldn't hide her concern.

'Tha' looks as tho' tha's sin a ghost, Peter,' she cried.

'Nay, old girl,' came his shaken reply, as he proceeded to tell his tale. 'Not seen, but heard!'

When he'd finished recalling his grim account, Lidia walked to the chair and knelt to the level of her husband's face.

'I don't think tha's heard any such ghoul; it's thy wig. Tha's burnt half of the right side off with thy candle!'

'Oh, praise be to God,' exclaimed the relieved sexton, and he resolved to dispose of the wig first thing the next day.

The exterior of the tower, with its lofty spire, is probably the landmark most familiar to Wakefield folk and regular visitors to the city. It was reported that when restoration work was undertaken in the nineteenth century, work that saw the spire removed for repairs, some passengers aboard steam trains approaching Wakefield stations refused to believe they had arrived at their destination when they discerned no tower, no spire and no weathervane on the horizon. It was during these periods of renovation when a number of notable events occurred.

George H. Crowther, giving a short account of 'this ancient and important town' in an 1886 publication, described how the original height of the spire exceeded 125 feet, its walls being 10 inches thick. In 1715, strong winds blew away a third of the spire, with the weather vane similarly falling victim to the gale. The subsequent rebuilding work was considered satisfactory until 1802, when it was found that further repairs would be required. Then in 1823, an inspection of the tower was ordered.

In June that year scaffolding was installed around the spire and the weathervane was removed. The vane was described as looking like a 'farm-yard poultry cock' by Wakefield writer John Hewitt, who, in 1862, published the first volume of his legendary and apparently incomplete series, *The History & Topography of the Parish of Wakefield and its Environs*, the final volume of which ends on page 402 in the middle of a sentence about Sandal Castle! Hewitt's writing, less known than Walker's, offers a more personal insight into Wakefield's history, complete with poetry, vivid reflection and perhaps not a little colourful conjecture. The volumes themselves, in their original form (the city library possesses a photocopy of the majority of pages in modern binding), are complete with several pages of coloured adverts describing the wares of Wakefield traders, such as Thomas Hawley of 152 Westgate, who manufactured and sold Scott's 'celebrated' Wakefield biscuits. There was also Henry Walker's garment dying, cleaning and scouring business at Tavern and Legh Streets at Primrose Hill in the town; John Todd's premises at Crown Court, Chancery Lane, where Mr Todd sold barometers, thermometers, galvanic machines and batteries, books, time pieces and philosophical lamps; and notices advertising Mr Hewitt's own business, for he was a fancy goods dealer at 72 Westgate. Hewitt offered all manner of services including letterpress printing, tickets for steam ships bound for New York, 'Christmas Amusements' and, 'coming in February 1864', a 'large and choice stock of French and English valentines and poetry cards'. Enumerated in the 1871 census, John Hewitt, then residing at Horbury, recorded that he was 'author of the History of Wakefield, miscellaneous poems &c., newspaper reporter, news & shipping agent, hair dresser, perfumer, and tea and tobacco dealer'. His continuing series of Wakefield history was reviewed in the July–December 1866 volume of *Notes and Queries: A medium of inter-communication for literary men, general readers, etc.* The reviewer described Hewitt as a 'tradesman in comparatively humble circumstances, and entirely self-educated' who wrote with enthusiasm about his native town. The critic went on to remark that though Hewitt 'occasionally falls into ludicrous mistakes and peculiarities of style, he nevertheless manages to present his readers with a great deal of interesting local matter which would otherwise fall into oblivion.'

For all his eccentricities, Hewitt's accounts of the spire (and a great many other Wakefield topics) are worthy of note. He remembered how the weathervane, after it was removed in 1823, was taken on a tour of the town's streets, with this curious parade set to music as a band accompanied the procession, treating the assembled crowds to their favourite tunes. An eminent Hull-based architect, Charles Mountain, who added the impressive façade to Beverley Guildhall in 1832, came to Wakefield to carry out the inspection. He recommended that the steeple be restored to its original height, and Hewitt recalled that the work was completed by that October. With some sadness Hewitt remarked that the weathercock was replaced by an arrow, but this did not carry out its purpose, becoming stuck. Before the scaffolding was taken down, Hewitt said that on 10 October, an Altofts maltster, Joseph Dennison, climbed the structure and ascended to the very top of the steeple. There he 'cleverly performed several dangerous feats of agility, such as standing upon his head, at the top of one of the scaffold poles!' Hewitt's memories also included witnessing a band who assembled in the same place to play what he described as sweet music which 'resounded most charmingly through the mid-air'. But later that century, more work would be required to improve the spire.

An engraving of the spire of All Saints' Church, from George H. Crowther, 1886.

Wakefield Cathedral tower and spire.

On 4 April 1857, the *Leeds Times* ran the following report:

THE SPIRE OF THE PARISH CHURCH – We are glad to find that some steps are being taken to render the beautiful spire of this church perfectly safe – a condition in which it has not been for the last twenty years. A public meeting of the inhabitants was held on Wednesday, in the vestry, for the purpose of taking preliminary measures for repairing the tower of the edifice, taking down and re-building the spire, and for re-searing the body of the church, &c. The Rev the Vicar presided, and after stating the desirability of accomplishing the above objects, an estimate of the cost was laid before the meeting, showing that the amount required would be about £8,000, which it was proposed to raise by public subscription. After some discussion, the meeting adjourned until the 16th instant, at which time the Bishop of Ripon is expected to be in attendance. The Vicar and Church-wardens were chosen as a committee for the time being, with power to add to their number.

The architect, George Gilbert Scott, soon to be knighted, was appointed by the committee and asked to produce a report recommending exactly what restoration work he felt should be undertaken. As part of his findings, he advised the committee to remove the spire. For a time, after the tower had been re-cased in stone, the new tower was topped by the old spire.

In March 1860, scaffolding was duly erected, and the *Leeds Intelligencer* reported, in August that year, that the contractor was 'very diligently pursuing the task of erecting a very handsome spire on the parish church, so that the distinctive mark of Wakefield, which has long been missed by passers-by, will, we believe, very shortly be restored in its pristine beauty and dimensions.' The publication went on to convey the hope that the work would be completed apace and 'public spirit will not long suffer the somewhat incongruous spectacle of a new spire tacked to an old edifice.'

The temptation of climbing the scaffolding was too great for some, and the site became a veritable fairground attraction as townsfolk competed to execute the most daring, dangerous and daft stunts. Soon the final stone of the old spire was removed, and the first stone of the new one was laid by Mrs Camidge, the vicar's wife. A new weathervane was installed, another farmyard cock, within which was placed a piece of parchment, upon which, Hewitt claimed, was written the names of local officials. Before the scaffolding was entirely taken away, some adventurous folk climbed it to mount the weathervane. The *Leeds Times* reported on 11 May 1861, under the headline 'FOOLHARDINESS', how even after the final piece of scaffold had been removed, a couple of workmen, determined to ascend to the summit, climbed up the crockets and descended without injury to their persons. The newspaper explained that 'their rash adventure has excited a great deal of indignation in the town' and Hewitt wrote that thousands had borne witness to it.

No doubt many of these onlookers were present when a Wakefield hairdresser, George Roberts, a married man in his fifties who lived at Red Lion Yard, Kirkgate, took a customer, William Abson, a Wakefield joiner, to the top of the steeple. At the summit, Mr Roberts proceeded to shave the man, who was positioned precariously upon an upturned bucket!

The new weathercock, like its predecessor, failed in its purpose and refused to move, so in July 1862 it was removed and made heavier. The job of bringing it down and replacing it fell to three steeplejacks from Manchester. The men were skilled in the art of kite flying and as they proceeded to remove the weathercock, they gave the folk of Wakefield, who'd taken to the streets in great numbers, a fine aerial exhibition. The steeplejacks tied a rope to the highest stone of the church steeple and guided their kite on a mid-air route that took in Northgate, Westmorland Street, Teal Street, Westgate and Southgate, with the purpose of securing the rope tightly around the steeple. By using a pulley system and a small wooden seat, the men took down the weathercock within just twenty minutes, replacing it the following Tuesday. Though they made it look easy, ascending and descending the building in this way was a serious business. Thankfully, nobody came to any harm on that occasion, but this was not always so.

On 4 August 1892, the *York Herald* ran a story titled 'SHOCKING DEATH OF A STEEPLE JACK AT WAKEFIELD'. A Huddersfield man was working on a chimney at Marriott's worsted mill at Balne Lane when brickwork gave way and he fell the distance of 57 feet, and was found 'quite dead' in a weaving shed.

A similar incident was reported in December 1899 when the *Western Times* told of the death

Even in the days before proper consideration was given to safety at work, the precarious positions taken by these men must have turned the stomachs of those watching below.

of two men who fell 200 feet from scaffolding that broke under their feet while they were removing the final stone from the top of a chimney stack at Wakefield Prison.

Today, safely secured fundraisers take to the spire and abseil to the ground in return for donations, which are gifted to a variety of charities and the Cathedral restoration fund.

The restoration overseen by Gilbert Scott was finally completed in 1886, though some of the work was finished by 1874, when a reopening ceremony was held on Wednesday, 3 November. It was described by a correspondent from the *Sheffield Daily Telegraph*:

In the morning there was a celebration of the Holy Communion, at which 104 communicants were present. Shortly after eleven o'clock in the forenoon a procession was formed at the Church

Abseiling at the Cathedral in 2014. *By courtesy of Terry Rochford.*

Institute and moved along the crowded streets to the Church. The procession consisted of the Borough and West Riding magistrates and their clerks, the borough member (Mr T.K. Sanderson), the mayors of Wakefield and Pontefract, the clergy, the choir, the Restoration Committee, the clerk of works, the contractors, the gentry, &c. The church, which presented a magnificent appearance, was crammed in every part, and hundreds of persons were unable to gain admission. The service, which occupied exactly two hours, was of a most interesting character, and the musical portion of it was admirably rendered by a choir of between forty and fifty voices under the direction of Fred Dykes, Esq. A lengthy, eloquent, and most appropriate sermon was preached by the Bishop of Ripon from the first verse of the 122nd Psalm. At the close of a most interesting and impressive service a collection was made towards a debt of about £2,000 on the restoration fund, and no less than £218 was realized. At two o'clock in the afternoon an excellent public luncheon was provided in the saloon of the Corn Exchange. The Bishop of Ripon presided, and there was an influential gathering, consisting of between 400 and 500 ladies and gentlemen. The Bishop proposed the usual loyal toasts, and a number of complimentary toasts were given. In the course of the proceedings Mr R.B. Mackie promised to give £250 towards the extinction of the debt of £2,000, Mr T.K. Sanderson promised £100, and Mr Haigh, the Mayor, £50. In the afternoon there was a sale of work by the teachers, at the Church Institute, and in the evening another service was held in the church.

The final improvements to the ancient building were seen in October 1886. As part of the changes and new work, the vestry was removed to the northeast end, walls and buttresses were rebuilt, the old north and south galleries were removed (traces of these can be seen today) and work was undertaken on the then east window.

In September 1886, the *Liverpool Mercury* reported that the restoration had been ongoing for 'a quarter of a century at intervals, and during that period about £30,000 has been expended in improving the interior and exterior of the grand old edifice, which will, it is expected, very shortly become the cathedral for the new diocese of Wakefield.' That prediction came true and the diocese was officially established on 18 May 1888, before being controversially disbanded on 20 April 2014, when it was swallowed up by the new Diocese of West Yorkshire and the Dales, which covers an area of 2,425 square miles and serves over two million people. But back in September 1886, when the report appeared in the Liverpool newspaper, the Wakefield churchwardens were busy witnessing the finishing touches to the lengthy restoration.

On 16 September, work was completed on one of the south buttresses that had been rebuilt. When this had been taken down in preparation for the new work, Crowther reported that the contractors discovered 'two small oblong copper plates'. They measured about 6 inches by 4 inches and had apparently been inserted in 1725. Upon the plates were engraved the name of the vicar of that time, a Reverend Scott, the eight churchwardens who served, and the name of the then church sexton, William Briggs, who was a predecessor to Peter Priestley. So on that day in September 1886, to mark the completion of the new buttress, a similar gesture was made. A bottle was placed in the stonework containing copies of the most recent editions of the *Wakefield Herald*, the *Wakefield Express*, the *Yorkshire Post* and, according to Crowther, the latest parish church guide and church accounts. Also in the bottle was a statement written by two officials from the Registry Office, named Mr Graham and Mr Hall. It began:

> In the name of God Amen,
>   In the month of September in the year of our Lord Christ one thousand and eight hundred and eighty-six and in the fiftieth year of the reign of her most Gracious Majesty Victoria (D.G.) Queen of Great Britain and Ireland, and Empress of India, this scroll is deposited in commemoration of the restoration of eleven buttresses and other stone work on the south side of the Parish Church of Wakefield.

As it continued, the statement gave the names of those who'd paid for the work, they being worsted manufacturer Major Joseph Barker, of Holme Field, Thornes (later becoming Holmfield park), and Sir Lionel Pilkington, of Chevet, and the document explained that the work on the buttresses completed the 'general restoration of the tower, spire, south porch, windows, organ, new vestry, and oaken stalls in place of pews'.

Much upset was caused in recent years when congregants and other local people learned that new, removable seating, in the form of wooden chairs, was to replace the oaken stalls, which had been installed in 1874. Letters were written to the press, and the Cathedral website advertised the sale of the said pews (in actual fact these were the oaken stalls just mentioned). It might seem doubtful that the Wakefield folk of Victorian times felt similar dismay when their church seating was changed, for the 'pews' of the day, which the stalls had just replaced, and were described (in an 1876 statement concerning subscriptions made towards the restoration work) as old and unsightly. The modern Wakefield clergy made this argument at the time of the most recent change, suggesting that the proposed moveable seating improved upon that which was being removed, just as had been the case in the 1870s, when nobody had complained.

However, similar opposition to that heard in recent times was reported in the local press during the nineteenth century, as seen by a report that appeared in the *Leeds Intelligencer* on 5 August 1848:

WAKEFIELD PARISH CHURCH

An attempt is being made to have the pews in the parish church removed, and stalls put in the place of them. This step has been strongly opposed by many of the pew-owners, and a good deal of bad feeling has resulted from the controversy.

The protestors won a reprieve at that time, but the pews were eventually taken away, and in 1876 the eventual new stalls were said to be 'handsome open seats of oak, with carved ends'. It was these stalls that were taken out as part of the restoration of the nave in 2013.

The 1886 statement in a bottle went on to pronounce that the new church was dedicated to the glory of Almighty God 'and the free use of all devout worshippers' in what was an 'edifice suitable for a Cathedral Church for the first Bishop of Wakefield who, it is trusted, will be appointed next year.' During the lengthy restoration, Sir George Gilbert Scott, who had been first entrusted with compiling a report and carrying out work on the building back in 1857, passed away, eight years before the work was finally completed. He was remembered at the end of the 1886 statement:

This work completes the undertaking commenced in 1857, on the report of the late Sir Gilbert Scott, and the memorial thus consigned to the safe custody of stone and mortar will be confirmation strong to some future antiquarian as to the circumstances under which the present restoration has taken place.

One aspect of the old parish church that has never been restored is the jackdaws that once lived in the tower. They were known as 'Sharp's pigeons', after Reverend Sharp, who used to preach at the church. Hewitt reckoned to have regularly counted at least twenty of the birds perched upon the weathervane and claimed that locals who captured the birds and attempted to domesticate them had to clip the creatures' wings to prevent them from flying back to the steeple for a reunion with their friends. By the time Hewitt published the second volume of his Wakefield history, the new steeple of the 1860s had been installed but the birds had not returned. To lament their loss, Hewitt penned the following verse:

> *The Daws from here have flown away,*
> *No longer round the Steeple play;*
> *We know not where they fly or roam,*
> *The re-built Steeple's not their home!*

As recently as 2015, a peregrine falcon with chicks made its home on the cathedral tower, but 200 years ago it was a bird of a different kind that performed an astonishing feat in Wakefield. The year was 1811, and a local daredevil advertised his intention to fly from the battlements of the church all the way to the bowling green at Southgate, a distance of about a quarter of a mile. Henry Clarkson recalled this birdman in his recollections of a long life lived in the town (*Memories of Merry Wakefield*, first edition published in 1887). He wrote how the man attached a rope to the battlements, driving a stake through the other end at a bowling green. He then climbed to the top of the church tower, and using his rope as a zip wire, hurled himself into the air, flying over the roofs and houses of the town below. Gathered spectators were thrilled as he flapped his arms and soared across the sky, the illusion of flight firmly imprinted in the imaginations of the crowd. Clarkson assured his readers that the man achieved a safe landing!

Opposite the west door of the church stands Bread Street, known in early days as Bread Booths, or Ratten Row, a reminder of the fourteenth-century bakehouse that once stood at the west end of the street. Citizens were not allowed to bake bread for profit without a licence and so were compelled to use the manorial facility, which was only removed in 1860 when the former Church Institute was built (opening in 1862). The site is now marked by a blue plaque. Many of the bakers operated booths on Bread Street, the name adopted in 1837. Also on the street was the Cross Keys Inn, which supplied the church with its sacramental wine for the Lord's Supper. In 1743 and 1764, the presiding Archbishop of York (Thomas Herring, then Robert Hay Drummond) requested certain information from the parishes in his charge. According to the responses from Wakefield, communion was performed at the church more frequently than in most Yorkshire parishes, so large quantities of wine were required. And in very early days, chantry priests occupied houses on the street.

The street is now somewhat run down and mainly used by people looking for easy access to the shops on Northgate, the cathedral, the Ridings on Kirkgate, or by customers accessing the Black Rock Pub by the back door. But behind the bread booths, and under the old structures that once stood in place of their current counterparts, it is rumoured that there existed a hidden pathway of interconnected arched cellars leading to and from the parish church. These cellars, still in place, are now firmly fixed in Wakefield myth and folklore, but is there any evidence for the existence of any such underground passage?

In his 1824 book, *An Historic Sketch of the Parish Church, Wakefield*, Reverend J.L. Sisson wrote that twenty-four chantry priests belonged to the church and each of these priests had lodgings in houses to the north of the churchyard, namely in Northgate and Bread Street, known in Sisson's time as Ratten Row, and in the time of the priests as Bread Booths.

Writing about the old religious houses in Bread Street, Hewitt expanded on the link between the street and the church:

A nineteenth-century photograph of Bread Street, with the sign of the Cross Keys Inn on the right.

In bygone times, it was customary to erect booths for the sale of bread at the front of houses in Bread Street, and from that cause this street was called 'Bread Booths' and afterwards its present name.

… where now stands the Mitre Inn, was a Priest's residence. Several other residences of Priests were also in the same locality; and from that circumstance, and the number of people who came to the Church and the Priests' houses, the Bread Booths were erected for the purpose of selling in them bread both to the Priests and their friends.

A subterranean passage was formerly connected with this old house. It led from one of the cellars in the direction of the Parish Church. The entrance to it is now walled up. The passage was arched over with bricks, and about 6ft in height. Probably, this underground road was for the priests to proceed by its means to and from this building and the church.

It is believed that this old house has been used as a secret Church in days of persecution.

Henry Clarkson described how entry to the churchyard was obtained in the days of his childhood. Specifically referring to the years 1810 and 1811, he explained:

At that time, the Parish Church yard was much smaller than it is now, a range of houses and shops being continued from Northgate, partly standing in the present street, and partly in the

A watercolour of Bread Street by Wakefield artist Louisa Fennell in 1900. *By courtesy of WLSL.*

Church yard; these buildings completely blocked up the whole west side of the Church yard, extending as far as opposite the George Hotel, and the last house at that end was occupied by Wakefield Dispensary. The principal entrance to the Church yard, was an ordinary archway, under the centre of the houses I have described, about where the present west gateway is now.

Walker commented further on the arched passage. He wrote of a house adjoining a Mr Bucktrout's grocer's shop, whose descendant, Jerimiah Bucktrout, advertised for sale his Seville oranges, perfect for use in wine making, in the local press in the early 1800s. A George Bucktrout, as will be seen, is connected to another story about Wakefield passages, but in this one Bucktrout appears because his shop adjoined a house occupied by a John Bagshaw, a scissors grinder. Walker revealed that beneath Bagshaw's house was 'a low archway entrance to the churchyard opposite Bread Street'.

Many of the houses that stood before the entrance to the churchyard, an entrance that is still used today to access the building via the west door (known as the tower entrance), were cleared away in 1821. Sisson told his readers that the inhabitants were to be especially praised for helping to knock down their houses to improve the vista.

Looking down Bread Street in 1884, with derelict properties dominating the scene. *By courtesy of YAHS.*

Several nineteenth-century deeds deposited at the Registry of Deeds on Newstead Road in Wakefield contain specific references to arched cellars under Bread Street, which are described as being in 'parts', with each part then in the possession of the occupants of the individual properties and each one adjoining the cellar of the building next door. One such deed refers to the purchase of a building on Bread Street by Alfred Moodie, a wine merchant who, until recently, was remembered by the name of a bar called 'Moody's' on Little Westgate (backing on to Bread Street). In the deed, a reference is made to the purchase of the building by a James Wells from an Elizabeth Hardcastle in 1812, and an earlier transaction, which took place in 1791, involving Wells and a Mr Liversidge, is also recorded. Reference is also made to plans drawn up in 1866, and to an indenture from 1853. All of these deeds contain the following passage: 'and also that part of the arched cellars under Bread Street otherwise Ratten Row aforesaid adjoining upon the same premises.' Perhaps a little excavation could reveal once and for all what lies, or perhaps what doesn't lie, beneath Wakefield.

For many centuries ecclesiastical courts sat in judgement of the humble man and woman. Slander was one of the common charges heard, and sexual slander was regularly dealt with.

Bread Street in 2015.

In 1850, the Richmond Ecclesiastical Court heard such a charge, and it was one that attracted national attention. It concerned Joseph Horner, an outspoken Wakefield corn miller who, as a non-conformist worshipper, vehemently opposed paying church rates, and no doubt resented having to pay to grind his corn at the Wakefield Soke Mills. The soke was a feudal custom of medieval times that had lingered during the nineteenth century, compelling millers to grind their corn within the soke mills (at a charge), and brought their lessee great profits. The soke was finally abolished in the second half of the century; but until 1853 it was alive and well, and the lessees at the time were Jose Luis Fernandes and his brother, Nowell Luis Fernandes, who campaigned long and hard to avoid losing their soke rights.

Back in 1850, Mr Horner had got into trouble for repeating a rumour about the Fernandes brothers' sister, who had been due to marry a respected Wakefield merchant. The match was ultimately called off and Miss Fernandes retired from the town to console herself. A story had got about that she was pregnant, and this, it was said, was why she had fled! Horner, who was in his seventies and himself well known in the town, was heard passing on this allegation to a friend of his.

The Fernandes family demanded that Horner substantiate his claim, but of course he had no evidence for it and had only told his friend what he'd heard. A suit was brought against him, which was heard by the court in Richmond. On hearing the particulars, the court found in favour of Miss

The Soke Mill shown from Wakefield Bridge in 1884. *By courtesy of YAHS.*

Fernandes and told Horner he must perform penance in the parish church at Wakefield on Sunday, 25 August 1850. He must have burned with humiliation at the mere thought.

Horner was head of a firm employing fifty-two males and three females; being so well known, large crowds gathered early in the morning outside his home at Red Lion Yard, Kirkgate, on the day of his punishment. Mr Abson, the daring hairdresser, may well have been present, for he and his widowed mother were Horner's next-door neighbours. The assembly was so large in number (some reports suggested there were many thousands), that those present formed a procession from Horner's door to the parish church. A few had no doubt come to gloat, or gawp at the elderly widower's fall from favour, whilst a great many others were sympathetic to the old man. These sympathizers walked beside Mr Horner as he made his way, with his son and namesake, Joseph Horner junior, to the Corn Exchange at the top of Westgate, the building that had replaced an older Corn Exchange in 1838. Just before twelve o'clock, they were addressed by Horner's son, who had climbed the lamppost in front of the building so that he might be heard by all:

> Respected friends, it cannot but afford my father and his family the highest pleasure, in this our day of trial, to see so many of his neighbours and friends assembled to sympathize, encourage and support us through this trying occasion. It is almost needless for me to say, as you are all aware, that my father is the last man who would have perpetrated anything calculated to injure either the person, property, or character of any individual, high or low, rich or poor, and especially a young lady. He has lived amongst you all his life, and is now seventy-one years of age. My father is guilty of telling the rumour he heard to one individual, but the story had become popular property, and was believed to be truth. However, as soon as my father heard that friends of Miss Fernandes were about to take proceedings against him for setting the story agoing, he called upon the family, offering any apology either oral or written, and, by way of atonement for his part in the affair, to pay £30 to any charitable institution in the town; but all would not avail, and I am sorry to say that we have today to desecrate the Sabbath and the temple of God, our beautiful parish church, by one of those semi-absurd customs of a semi-barbarous age, and which I hope the present enlightened age will ere long extinguish. My friends, although my father is aged, he is in good spirits, and will be enabled to go through this ordeal with firmness. Let us not commit ourselves this day, but let us be peaceable and quiet, and reverence the day by a proper deportment. The Vicar has done all he could to prevent these scandalous proceedings, and to him and every one of our friends, I tender, for my father, my best thanks, and forgiveness to our persecutors.

The speech went down well, and Horner's supporters cheered and clapped loudly as the man reappeared on the steps of the Corn Exchange. They accompanied him down Little Westgate until he made it to the south frontage of the church. The windows of the shops and houses on his route were occupied by well-wishers waving handkerchiefs and improvised banners. At length he appeared at the eastern steps and as he made his way through the churchyard, packed with ever more supporters, somebody shouted out the name Fernandes and it was met by howls and groans of derision.

It was later revealed that the vicar, Reverend Samuel Sharp, had lobbied for the penance to be carried out in the vestry, away from the congregation, after lessons had been read, thus avoiding a probable riot in the nave. The doors, which had been shut firmly during the twenty minutes or so that the penance lasted, were opened to reveal an ashen-faced Mr Horner, whose reappearance was met by more cheers and applause.

The Fernandes family weren't without their own controversies, and in 1861 Jose Luis Fernandes was committed to York Prison on a charge of contempt of court after he refused to answer questions when called as a witness on the grounds his answers might incriminate him. The case concerned the recent borough election in Wakefield and charges of bribery against his friend, John Barff Charlesworth. But that affair is very much another story for another day!

Hewitt enjoyed advertising his Christmas amusements in his Wakefield publications and it seems from his vivid accounts of the festive period that there was much amusement to be had during Wakefield Christmases of olden times. Sword dancers, or rapier dancers, as Hewitt termed them, (who were generally young men), formed troupes and used to go about Wakefield in fancy dress, knocking on the doors of the homes of their friends and performing their apparently dangerous, yet intricate, steps as well as little dramas, such as the Robin Hood ballads and an old mumming play entitled *The Peace Egg*, which Hewitt seemed to find very tiresome indeed.

Another Christmas custom was that of throwing dried yule logs, or clogs, to give them their proper West Riding name, on to the fire on Christmas Eve. In 1777 John Brand published a book titled *Observations on Popular Antiquities, chiefly illustrating the origin of our vulgar customs, ceremonies and superstitions.* In his book he explained the tradition of burning wooden 'Christmas Candles' of an uncommon size, and the laying of 'a log of wood upon the fire, called a Yule-Clog or Christmas-Block, to illuminate the house, and, as it were, turn night into day. This custom is in some measure still kept up in the North of England.'

The English poet Robert Herrick, who lived from 1591 to 1674, wrote a poem about Christmas ceremonies, published in the 1640s, in which the following verse referred to the custom still practised at Wakefield in Hewitt's day:

Come, bring with a noise,
My merry, merry boys,
The Christmas log to the firing;
While my good dame, she
Bids ye all be free,
And drink to your hearts' desiring.

With the last year's brand
Light the new block, and
For good success in his spending
On your psaltries play,

That sweet luck may
Come while the log is a-teending.

Drink now the strong beer,
Cut the white loaf here;
The while the meat is a-shredding
For the rare mince-pie,
And the plums stand by
To fill the paste that's a-kneading.

Brand felt that the yule clog custom dated to a time long before Christmas was ever celebrated in England, probably being a Winter Solstice tradition; so who knows how long the hearths of Wakefield had burned clogs into embers? Hewitt maintained that whilst he was not a superstitious man he always liked to keep a yule clog handy, and he insisted that on Christmas Eve, 'most of the people of Wakefield and the neighbourhood burn Yule Clogs.'

Bringing in the Yule Log, or Clog, on Christmas Eve, from *Observations on Popular Antiquities*, first published in 1777.

Wakefield from the Town Hall in 1880, showing the parish church. *By courtesy of YAHS.*

Wakefield Cathedral in the early twentieth century, showing the east end extension of 1904.

A stranger practice concerning the word yule was also described by Hewitt. He claimed that during bygone Christmases, much dancing took place within the walls of the parish church after prayers. He reckoned the dancing congregants accompanied their moves by 'singing and crying aloud Yole! Yole! Yole!' His reasoning for the said custom was that in Old English, he thought Yule, or yole, meant evil, and by crying out the word while dancing, evil was thus banished. Brand insisted that 'yule' was a primitive word for the revolution of a wheel, and cited the Venerable Bede as his source. He explained that the wheel was common both to the festivals held at summer and winter solstices, the former being symbolic of the return of the sun after the winter solstice at yuletide.

So, with the performing swordsmen, yule clog merriment and parish church dancing, Christmas at Wakefield must have been a time looked forward to by all.

Chapter Two

Northgate, the Bull Ring, Wood Street and the Civic Area

Exactly 700 years ago, on 'Friday next after the Octave of the Ascension, in the 9th year of the reign of King Edward, son of King Edward', or otherwise 12 June 1316, the court of the manor of Wakefield sat to deal with matters that had arisen since it last convened three weeks earlier. One of these matters concerned the distribution of land on the lord of the manor's waste at Bichill, otherwise Bitch Hill or Beech Hill. This place stood next to Butcher Row, a street that was close to the Bull Ring.

Several individuals paid the court for leave to take certain pieces of land on the site. Henry Bele gave two shillings for a piece opposite his house. Bele's land measured 38 feet long by 16 feet

Northgate seen from opposite the parish church in 1885. *By courtesy of YAHS.*

Looking down Northgate in 2015.

wide. Nicholas Carter's son, William, also paid two shillings for a plot 25 feet by 16 feet in size. Gregory Mercer paid the same sum for a smaller piece of the land that measured 14 feet by 9 feet and lay opposite John Kyde's booth, whilst married couple Thomas and Margaret Aleyn paid for a plot located opposite the booth of Adam, son of Laurence. The Aleyn's plot was 36 feet by 16 feet. Richard Man, who paid just twelve pence, took a plot right at the end of Henry of Swillington's old booth, measuring 20 feet by 10 feet. There was one more piece of the land to deal with that day, and this was bought by Robert Hade and his wife, Matilda, with the purpose (it has been argued by Walker, Richard Bell, et al.) of building a decent sized house there between the Aleyn's booth and Philip Damyson's booth. Robert and Matilda's newly acquired plot measured 30 feet by 16 feet, and it was to be held for themselves and their heirs, with a yearly payment of sixpence to be made to the court over three instalments within each twelve-month period.

Nineteenth-century antiquarian Reverend Joseph Hunter, who wrote a history of South Yorkshire, comprising a two-volume set that fetches a pretty penny at auction today, and Wakefield's own J.W. Walker, were among several historians who argued that this Robert Hade and his wife Matilda were really the Robin Hood and Maid Marion of the famous ballads and popular folklore. It should be noted that in this period the same Wakefield court rolls named Robert Hoods of Newton and Alverthorpe. And there also exists a much earlier twelfth-century reference to a fugitive named Robert Hood, who appeared in the records of York Assizes in 1225.

This earlier Hood had made the decision not to attend court and consequently his goods were confiscated and he was outlawed. Was he the basis for the nickname Robehod, subsequently given to outlaws appearing in medieval court rolls? Who knows; but the supposed evidence identifying Wakefield's early fourteenth-century Robert Hade as the Lincoln green-clad outlaw seems to be as follows.

A year after Robert and Matilda paid their fee to the court for the land at Bichill, Edward II gifted the manor of Wakefield with Sandal Castle to Thomas, Earl of Lancaster, in order to settle a dispute between Lancaster and John, Earl of Warenne, the then lord of the manor. The dispute had arisen when Lancaster's wife, Alice de Lacy, was kidnapped from Lancaster's Pontefract Castle by one of Warenne's men. She was taken, apparently without putting up much of a fight, to Sandal Castle, which Lancaster then promptly laid siege to, burning the castle's defences. Scorch marks attributed to the siege were discovered during twentieth-century excavations carried out at the site.

Louisa Fennell's 1904 watercolour of Butcher Row. *By courtesy of WLSL.*

In 1322, Lancaster, who had, a decade earlier, been instrumental in the beheading of the King's favourite, Piers Gaveston, called to arms archers from his new manor of Wakefield. It's believed that Robert Hood of Wakefield answered the call because his name was not recorded in the court rolls among those fined for failing to rally to their lord's demand. With his archers dressed in Lincoln green, Lancaster marched the thousand-strong force to Boroughbridge, where, on 16 March 1322, they were hemmed in by Sir Andrew Harclay's soldiers, who were fighting for the King. A battle took place and Lancaster was defeated, humiliated, and ultimately executed a few days later, following a mock trial before a kangaroo court, at his own Pontefract Castle.

A couple of years later, the Sheriff of Nottingham was commissioned to confiscate land from those who had fought for Lancaster, men dubbed as Contrariants. In his 1944 book, *The True History of Robin Hood*, J.W. Walker stated that those who had fled Boroughbridge with their lives were all outlawed, and some 'secreted themselves in woods … and turned their skill in archery against harmless passengers on the highroads, or against the deer in those forests.'

He went on to explain that the custodian of lands seized in Yorkshire was one Thomas de Eyvill, who had compiled a document, known as 'The Contrariants Roll', listing the confiscated lands in his possession. His roll recorded that rent had been received worth twenty-three pence for a five-chambered house, newly constructed on Bichill, Wakefield. Walker then took a leap of faith and determined that 'it seems almost certain that this building of five chambers was the dwelling-house that Robert and Matilda Hood erected on the 30 by 16 feet land on Bichill which they took from the lord of the manor on Friday next after the octave of the Ascension, 1316.'

Walker also drew his readers' attention to the Wakefield court rolls of 1357 and 1358, which, he claimed, contained the following entries:

> a tenement in Wakefield formerly in the tenure of Robert Hode lying on Bichill.
> … a messuage in Wakefield lying on Bichill on one side of a tenement formerly Robert Hoode's taken from the waste.

Other translations of these entries suggest they read differently, but still make reference to a tenement at Bichill, 'formerly of Robert Hode'. In the 1358 entry, Agnes, daughter of the Thomas Alayn, or Aleyn, named above, was recorded as paying twelve pence to the lord to take a messuage lying upon Bichill, which stood between the tenements formerly of Henry Bull and Robert Hode.

Walker's statement, 'it seems almost certain …', was certainly a bold one given that neither Robert Hood, nor indeed Robin Hood, were named in the Contrariants Roll, neither was there firm evidence to place a man of either name at the Battle of Boroughbridge, excepting the record that showed that such a named man wasn't fined for not answering the muster call. However, the notion that Robin Hood was from the Merrie City has certainly caught the imagination of several historians, Robin Hood enthusiasts, and indeed a former Member of Parliament for Wakefield, David Hinchcliffe. He tabled an Early Day Motion in 2004 that called for Nottinghamshire's claim to be 'Robin Hood County' to be dismissed, given the 'complete lack of any factual basis'. The motion stated that Robin was 'most likely to have been Robert Hode of Wakefield … recorded in the Wakefield Court Rolls as living with wife Matilda at Bichill, Wakefield, in 1316.' Hinchcliffe cited Robert's absence from the list of defaulters when Lancaster raised his army, ending his motion with the assertion that 'historical evidence indicates' that Robin Hood was a Yorkshireman. The motion was signed by twenty-nine Members of Parliament, including one Jim Hood, Labour Party member for Clydesdale.

The area in and around the Bull Ring, which Robert and Matilda called home, was also one of the sites of Wakefield's annual Winter Fair. This was one of many fairs and feasts once held in the town. John Hewitt gave an account of those still in existence in 1862 when he published the first volume of his history of Wakefield series.

Wakefield hosted several markets, with corn sold every Friday, fat cattle and sheep every Wednesday, lean cattle, sheep and pigs on both of those days, and a wool market held Wednesday to Friday. If hide and skin was desired, then Friday was the day to visit the town, and the Borough

Wakefield Borough Market in 1884, shown from the Town Hall. *By courtesy of YAHS.*

Market could be enjoyed on Fridays and Saturdays for the sale of 'Game, Poultry, Provisions, Farmers' and Gardeners' Produce, as well as Manufactured Articles'.

As for fairs and feasts, it seems that Wakefield enjoyed these in abundance, perhaps another reason for its Merrie City moniker. On 4 and 5 July, Wakefield Midsummer Fair offered the sale of horses on the first day and 'toys, pleasure, &c.' on the second. A similar fair was held in winter, when, on 11 November, horses were once more available for sale; and on the following day, toys and amusements were enjoyed, while the annual statutes for the hiring of male and female servants were held. The dates of the two fairs were altered if the first day happened to fall on a Sunday. This ancient custom meant that at Midsummer the first day was moved to the third of the month, and in winter, day one took place on 10 November.

Further afield, the once notorious – and still held – Lee Fair was a late summer attraction. Samuel Waters, in his book *Wakefield in the 17th Century*, cited a petition composed in 1656 by the people of West Ardsley to suppress the fair. Their petition described the event as 'utterly decayed' owing to the fact that a cloth market had been erected in Wakefield, which had taken the cloth trade away from the fair. The document further decried Lee Fair as a 'tumultuous meeting of the idle and loose persons of the Country, where there is much revelling and drunkenesse, and hath been noted these many yeares to be a meetinge where there is usually more or less bloodshed and some lives lost.' The petitioners suggested that the trifling produce on offer could be better supplied at the markets held each day at 'Leedes or Wakefield'.

Feasts were held at Ackworth and Ossett on Trinity Sunday; at Gawthorpe on the Wednesday, and Crofton and Sharleston hosted their own feasts in October. For those living in Horbury, Stanley-cum-Wrenthorpe, Thornes, Warmfield, Woodchurch, Crigglestone, Newmillerdam, East Ardsley, Woolley, Altofts, Wragby, Normanton and Sandal Magna, feasts were held throughout the year in these places.

A tradition that Hewitt claimed only died out in or about the 1820s concerned the ringing of the parish church bells at five o'clock in the morning on the first day of the Winter Fair. The bells were rung continuously for three hours, and a great bonfire 'kindled on the previous evening' burned brightly against the misty morning air so that the sound of the bells and the sight of the flames would draw the attention of parties heading to the fair with their cattle.

The fair, Hewitt explained, was held within the 'Bars of Wakefield', with cattle sold in Wakefield's public streets. The 'fat beasts occupied the whole of the ground from near the Theatre in Westgate to opposite the Parish Church. Fat bulls were shown near the Old Market-house, recently pulled down, and now the site of the Church Institute. The lean cattle were shown in the Bull Ring and

The Bull Ring in the mid-twentieth century, showing the original Strafford Arms, a posting house and hotel, which Charles Dickens described as 'one of the finest in the Kingdom'. It was built on land owned by the Earl of Strafford on the site of the former Black Swan hostelry, which was taken down in 1727.

The Strafford Arms, drawn by Henry Clarke. *By courtesy of WLSL.*

in Northgate.' It was an extensive event but became diminished when the Wakefield Cattle Market was begun, and even though in Hewitt's day lean cattle was still available for sale at the Winter Fair, it was no longer offered in the open streets, but at the cattle market instead, and in not so great a number.

Indeed, by 1845, it seems that the fair had fallen on hard times and was a shadow of its former glory, as a report from the *Leeds Intelligencer*, published on 15 November that year, testified:

WAKEFIELD FAIR. – The winter fair at Wakefield commenced on Tuesday morning last. The show of horses on that day was very small, and of an inferior kind. The statutes and pleasure fair was held on Wednesday. The hiring of servants was not very brisk, and the attendance of holiday lovers was much smaller than heretofore. Indeed the fair altogether was not so good, which may, no doubt, in a great measure be attributed to the circumstance of the place for holding it being so frequently changed, an arrangement injurious to the inhabitants generally.

Despite this appraisal, other papers reported that whilst the fair was generally poor, the public were treated to shows such as Hytlon's and Wombwell's travelling menageries, which gained notoriety as the century progressed. However, the *Leeds Times* made it known that of the other shows available at the Wakefield fair of 1845, there were 'none worth noticing'.

The Strafford Arms today, which replaced the building Dickens knew.

Just a couple of years later, the *Leeds Intelligencer* declared that the Winter Fair's 'pleasure fair was anything but pleasurable and it continued to rain without intermission during the whole of the afternoon,' whilst the 1843 offering was 'dull and unsatisfactory'. This decline was in evidence a decade earlier when the *Yorkshire Gazette* reported that although many servants had attended the 1833 fair, not many were hired, and tourists and the younger of the attendees were disappointed that only a single 'penny peep show' was offered by way of amusement.

Despite the event's apparent wane in quality, crowds continued to flock, and the *Leeds Times* on 19 November 1853 said that the fair, held on the Saturday and Monday, had brought a 'good mustering of sight-seers' who had patronized the traders but not the town's permanent stalls and shops. Once more, the horses on offer were disappointing, described as 'sorry specimens of horse-flesh', the paper declaring that 'this once important adjunct to our fair is fast falling into desuetude.' Pickpockets were in operation on the second day, but Wakefield was evidently well policed, and the thieves' attempts were quelled with little effort. The weather in Wakefield deteriorated the following day, and by the Wednesday a thick fog had descended on the town, with several accidents caused in consequence. Trains at Kirkgate Station were delayed, and as a result, papers due for sale at one in the afternoon did not arrive until four. Unable to see, passengers missed their footing on the platforms as they scurried about looking for somewhere to shelter in a station described by the Leeds paper as possessing inadequate accommodation. Perhaps the great fog was nature's way of drawing a veil over the previous days' proceedings.

The statutes continued to be held into the twentieth century, and the *Yorkshire Post*, reporting from the 1905 Winter Fair, stated that 'a large number of men and boys gathered in the Corn Market and offered themselves. Men asked £14 10s. to £26 10s. and boys £9 to £14 per year.' The higher sum was the equivalent of a £16,000 salary in today's money. The paper reported that few engagements were made.

Reports of Wakefield's Midsummer Fair were not much more encouraging, the *Bradford Observer* noting in 1843 that 'a great number of shows and bazaars, for the sale of fancy articles, were exhibited, but from the very limited attendance of the holiday people we fear they will meet with but poor encouragement.'

In contrast, Wakefield's Food, Drink & Rhubarb Festival, which is presently held in February each year, with stalls beginning in the Bull Ring and extending down the cathedral precinct, draws many visitors from across the country, including celebrity chefs and parties on organized coach excursions, keen to sample the famed delicacy grown in the heart of West Yorkshire's Rhubarb Triangle.

The 2016 festival on a wet Saturday afternoon, where many rhubarb-themed delicacies were on sale. Rhubarb grew in popularity in Yorkshire during Victorian times. On Leeds Provision Market in July 1874, a dozen bundles cost sixpence.

Away from the Bull Ring and along Northgate, near the swine and hog market, there once stood an old house that was believed to have contained a hidden chapel, or some primitive place of worship, used secretly during the Reformation. In late May 1756, work was being carried out on the house, which was owned by Joshua Dixon of Leeds. Thomas Binns, the builder, whose relations would continue in this trade in the town for many generations, had been hired to remove a false ceiling and plaster the adjoining wall. It was a hot and thirsty afternoon, and Binns was keen to complete his tasks for the day so he could return home and rest before starting another busy day the following morning.

In order to make his repairs, Binns had to remove wainscoting that was acting as a ceiling. Having carefully used his claw hammer and iron crow to take away the decorative oak panelling, the outlines of some figures, nestled in the cavity, suddenly caught his eye. Taking a closer look, Binns was astonished to discover dozens of statues and images, some of wood, others of alabaster, each strewn behind the wainscoting he'd just removed. He wasn't a pious man, but he read his Bible now and again and knew, as he carefully withdrew the items one by one, that they were religious icons, and he assumed they were of great value. He took some cloth that he used for wrapping around his tools, and gently placed this around the figures. Full of excitement, he finished plastering the wall and safely restored the panelling, before making his way home. That evening, talking to friends in the pub, he aroused great interest in his find, and by the same time the following day he'd made six pounds from making a show of them, charging each curious onlooker a penny a look. A week after Binns had happened upon his rare treasure, the *Leeds Intelligencer* heard about the discovery, and remarkably, an account of the report survives from the 8 June 1756 edition of the paper, given here in full:

> *Extract of a Letter from Wakefield, dated 5 June*
>
> Last Week as a Workman was making Alterations in an old Building (suppos'd to have been formerly a Popish Chapel), he concealed betwixt the Wall and Wainscot 46 Statues or Images, thought to have represented the Prophets, Apostles, &c. and three Bass relevio's [bas-reliefs] in Marble. 1st Represents Virgin Mary with a Book in her Hand teaching Jesus to read. 2nd Is thought to be one of the Popes giving Absolution to a Man from the Papal Throne. 3rd Is suppos'd a Representation of the horrid Manner of executing Hereticks, two different Ways, in the popish slaughter houses, the Inquisitions. On the second Marble is an Inscription, which I believe is not yet explained, tho' some in this Town have attempted it. It is imagined they have been concealed at the Reformation in the Reign of Henry VIII. By the careless position they lay in, their Concealment seems to have been done in a hurry, for fear of a Discovery by the Commissioners employed in the Reformation.
>
> The above Building is the Property of Mr Joshua Dixon of Leedes, which came by his Wife the Daughter of Mr Pith of this Town. The Workman made a rare Show of them and the first Day got six Pounds for a Sight of them at a Penny each Person.

Binns knew he was on to something but he hadn't the time to make public displays of his discovery, so he set about finding somebody to whom he could sell the figures. He thought of just the person. George Bucktrout, the local grocer, had a shop on Northgate and Binns was well aware that the grocer had an eye for religious fancies. He'd only the other week been preaching to the builder about some book he'd subscribed to a decade ago about the Scriptures, suggesting Binns might like to borrow it. He'd declined, but he knew his proposition would be met more positively by Bucktrout. And he was right. A price was agreed almost as soon as Bucktrout clapped eyes on Binns's figures. A dozen apples were probably a suitable deposit and Binns returned the next day to make the exchange.

The grocer then arranged for his sons to tend the shop and made straight for London, where he exhibited his new purchases before setting out on a tour of the provincial towns of the country. A year after the original discovery, Bucktrout placed an advert in the *Oxford Journal*, dated 5 February 1757:

WAKEFIELD ANTIQUE STATUES,

So justly admired by the CURIOUS

As Curiosities of this Sort are rarely to be met with, except in Palaces and Seats of the Nobility, who are at almost an incredible Expence in procuring them from abroad, it is not improper to publish the following short Account of these venerable Remains, which in some Measure will give the Public a faint Idea of what they have a favourable Opportunity of seeing in the greatest Perfection and highest Preservation, and at the same Time at so small an Expence.

Every Body knows to what a Height the Custom ran some Centuries ago in ornamenting Places of Worship with Sculpture and Painting, and what Sums were remitted from this Country into foreign Parts, and particularly ROME for the purchasing of Figures of this Kind.

Now as SANDAL CASTLE near WAKEFIELD then belonged to one of the first Families in the Nation, and it was near here that the great Battle was fought between the Houses of *York* and *Lancaster*, where the Duke of *York*, the Earl of *Rutland*, and others of the Nobility and Gentry were slain and K. *Edward* IV. not long after built a near Gothic Chapel on WAKEFIELD BRIDGE, in Remembrance of his Father, most of which is standing at this Time.

It is easy to conceive that such Places as these would not be without a Set of the richest Ornaments that could be got, and when the Chapels were abolished by King *Henry* VIII. the Figures would certainly have undergone the same Fate, had they not been secreted by the Monks and Friars, who 'tis imagined conveyed them from the Castle and the Chapel on the Bridge, thro' a subterraneous Passage, Part of which is now to be seen opening into a Cellar near the old Building where these very Statues were found, which was but an inferior Place of Worship, that was not expected to contain any Moveables of that Value. There is a dark Room in it called the Dungeon but these Curiosities lay concealed in the false Roof of the Chapel, where they had probably lain ever since the Reign of *Henry* VIII, somewhat more than 200 Years, and were at last discovered by a Workman that was going to do some Repairs in *May* last, 1756.

These Figures are now at the Sign of the *Chequer*, in the *High-street*, Oxford and are to be seen, without Loss of Time, from Nine in the Morning 'till Eight at Night, at *One Shilling* each.

N.B. Any Person who has seen once, may see them again with any of their Friends for Nothing.

Writing in a letter eleven years later, Reverend Benjamin Forster, a Lady Camden lecturer at the parish church in Wakefield, who lived at Alverthorpe Hall, spoke of 'a shopkeeper in this town, Bucktrout …' who sent the statues and figures 'to fairs all over the country, but the saints, indignant to be so degraded, estranged the minds of the *menu peuple* from the sight, so that the Sieur Bucktrout was not a gainer by the sacrilege.' The receiver of the letter, one Richard Gough, a noted antiquarian, profuse author, and director of the Society of Antiquaries of London, was keen to purchase the figures, or 'wooden gods' as he called them, for his 'lararium' or museum, and asked Reverend Forster to make enquiries of the grocer. Forster, who was more interested in when Gough was going to settle an outstanding bill for Stilton cheese that they'd had from an old lady from the town, replied that he would speak to Bucktrout, and that he would 'give sixpence for the Magazine which had a print of one of them.'

The magazine print in question is probably the one displayed, from the December 1756 edition of *The Gentleman's Magazine*, which shows, it has been suggested, an image of one of the alabaster figures found by Binns. It depicts St William of York, who became archbishop of the province in 1141.

The print, upon which its owner has written in ink 'an antique figure fd. at Wakefield', shows a monk at the feet of the archbishop with words in old French tumbling from his mouth. A letter to the magazine by one P. Gemsege (the pseudonym of Dr Samuel Pegge, the antiquary) described the circumstances surrounding the discovery of this and the other figures, just a few months earlier. The correspondent went on to suggest that the old French read '*S. Willam sanc price procures aydane*', which he translated as 'St William, you procure us help without meed or reward'. Gemsege reckoned there were actually twenty-five figures, rather than the forty-five reported in the days following the discovery.

St William of York.

Edward Parsons, in 1834, in *The Civil, Ecclesiastical, Literary, Commercial and Miscellaneous History of Leeds, Halifax, Huddersfield, Bradford, Wakefield* etc., described the statues in detail as:

representing Moses and Aaron, Kings David and Solomon, Christ, the twelve Apostles with their respective emblems, St Paul, St John the Baptist, and the three magi, Jasper, Melchior, Balthazar; St Ann, mother of the Virgin Mary, teaching her to read; St William, Archbishop of York, with his pastoral staff and mitre, and a monk at his feet praying; a figure with a mitre; a fine representation of two saints suffering martyrdom, in *alto relievo*, in alabaster; St John the Evangelist was represented in the cauldron surrounded by St Polycarp, St Ignatius, the principal Roman magistrates, and the executioners; and another group consisted of a saint lying on a board, whilst his intestines are twisted gradually out, by a spit turned round by two lictors.

The June 1759 edition of *The Gentleman's Magazine* included a print of the gruesome scene described above, though the caption suggested the saint was actually a bishop.

In the magazine, a writer calling himself Cantianus explained that he'd viewed the figures, his curiosity having been excited by Pegge's letter of a few years earlier, and again repeated the claim that the figures were found in the roof of an old Wakefield chapel, before being taken to London for exhibition. Norrison Scathcherd, in his essay on bridge chapels, first published in 1828, asserted that the figures must have originally come from the Chantry Chapel on Wakefield Bridge, rather than Sandal Castle, before being smuggled to safety in Northgate.

Thomas Binns would have been familiar with Wakefield's market cross that once stood in Cross Square, having been erected during the reign of Queen Anne, in about 1707. According to the art historian Nikolaus Pevsner, the architect was Theophilus Shelton, who, on 26 April 1704, was appointed as the first registrar of the West Riding Deeds Registry. The market cross was described in 1768 as a 'very elegant building, being an open colonnade of the Doric order supporting a dome, to which you ascend by an open circular pair of stairs in the centre of the building. This brings you to a room which receives light from a turret on the top, and may be called the town hall, for here they transact all their public business.'

It was built following an appeal by the townsfolk, who raised the required subscription in order that they might have a venue from which to sell, as Walker explained,

Representation of an ancient Bishop in the act of Martyrdom; from an ancient Carving on Wood.

'butter, eggs, poultry, etc.' and somewhere to hold meetings. Dairy and poultry were one thing, but this curious notice in the *Oxford University and City Herald* newspaper, dated 1 October 1814, suggests the sale of human beings as well: 'Thursday week, at the market-cross, Wakefield, Wm. Helam, of Thornhill, sold his wife for 5s. to John Blagg.' Hewitt also discussed this incident his book, suggesting frequent occurrences of such transactions. He claimed the seller was actually named William Heslam, who 'brought his wife' on Thursday, 13 September 1814 to the market cross, 'with a halter round her neck, and there publicly sold her to the best bidder!' He went on to say that Mrs Heslam 'was not very prizable', so small was the sum, and that 'the woman' enjoyed 'the fun and frolic heartily, and with greater pleasure than either the husband she had just left, (with the intention of thus being separated from him for ever), or the man who had just bought her as if she was an article of merchandize.' Hewitt concluded that 'numerous spectators were present

… the merriment of the lookers-on seemed to know no bounds.'

An earlier incident was noted in the *Leeds Intelligencer* on 15 February 1802:

On Saturday se'nnight, a private in the first West York Militia, quartered at Wakefield, led his wife by a halter to the market cross there, and sold her for five shillings, to a farmer of Cuffwell, in Nottinghamshire, who led away his prize in the presence of an exulting crowd.

The area around the market cross saw its fair share of trouble over the years before the cross was demolished in 1866 to much local despair and protest. On 7 November 1849, the *London Standard* told its readers about shocking scenes that had just unfolded in Wakefield. It was Guy Fawkes' Night on Monday, 5 November and the town had been brimming with excitement over the previous few days as they looked forward to the customary celebrations of that

The market cross shown in 1860. *By courtesy of YAHS.*

special evening. For many years the locals had collected kindling from their gardens and the heaths around the town, anything that would burn, to illuminate the Bull Ring with their enormous bonfires. A circle, many deep, would throng around the flames, and recently more and more spectators had joined in the fun. Drinking, singing and general merriment ensued, and each year the fires got taller, and the crowds grew wilder. In fact, things had been getting rather out of hand, and the newly formed Wakefield Borough Police force, inaugurated the previous September, was determined to put a stop to the much-loved festivities. As the parish church bells rang the seventh hour that evening, the plan swung into life and the entire force marched from their headquarters and headed for the Bull Ring. Their intention was simple: keep the area clear of revellers and no trouble would occur.

But it didn't work out at all how the police had hoped. Instead of meeting in the Bull Ring, the crowd, or 'mob' as the *London Standard* reporter termed them, had gathered in Cross Square, by the market cross. Word of the police's killjoy tactics had spread around the town earlier that day and the crowd had been whipped up into a frenzy by the more vocal ringleaders, who'd convinced the easily led that this was a mere glimpse of what was to come. Soon, they claimed, this newly assembled 'force' would be trampling all over their liberties. The police, it was decided, needed to be shown who ran this town, before they got too big for their shiny new boots.

Wakefield policemen of yesteryear.

Consequently, just a few minutes after the hour, somebody lit a barrel full of tar and a handful of men rolled it through the square towards the Bull Ring.

'See how they like that!' came the cry from the crowd.

The police flew into action and two of the ringleaders were immediately seized.

'RESCUE! RESCUE!' they cried out to their comrades, as policemen took hold of them.

A crowd greater than the officers had anticipated suddenly converged from all sides. But their savage kicks and punches did little to deter the policemen, who grabbed some of the more ragged rescuers by their shirt collars and proceeded to frogmarch them back to police station on King Street (originally known as the Police and Vagrant Office), where they could be dealt with appropriately. But the policemen couldn't get to safety fast enough, and outside the court house on Wood Street, realizing how hopelessly outnumbered they were, they drew their staves, and took the fight to the pumped-up hordes. Staves, however, were no match for 'stones, bricks, and missiles of all descriptions', which were 'hurled upon the officers like a storm of hail', according to the London newspaper.

One by one the officers fell, at least one losing consciousness. There was nothing else for it: they had to beat a hasty retreat. As soon as the policemen were inside their station, the troublemakers

The Bull Ring in 1880. *By courtesy of YAHS.*

The Bull Ring in the first few years of the 1900s.

returned to the great bonfire, but in somewhat smaller numbers, for the police had managed to return some of the violence, leaving casualties lying strewn in the streets around Northgate.

Later that evening, one man was discovered to have been a police spy, and as a last act of revenge he was set upon by the crowd. He only saved himself from probable murder when he spotted the door of the Boy and Barrel Inn (in the market place), through which he leapt to safety.

Back at the station, the police decided to bide their time. And just after eleven o'clock, they escorted the mayor, George William Harrison, to inspect the fires in the Bull Ring. They did so because word had reached them that the crowds had become bored, with many having returned to their homes, and surely nobody would dare to lay a finger on the mayor. But this was a false premise, for no sooner had the police returned when stones flew at them once again and they were surrounded. One missile knocked the mayor's hat off, and the chief constable was felled and 'trampled on'. Finally, at midnight, the aggressors gave up and order was restored at last.

There was further unrest in 1866, when it was decided, by the corporation, that the market cross was getting in the way of passing shoppers and street traffic. In their opinion, the time had come to sell it by public auction, on condition that the purchaser would be bound to remove the structure, thus creating much-needed space for access. But the corporation had either underestimated, or

Looking towards the Bull Ring from the bottom of Wood Street in 1885. *By courtesy of YAHS.*

didn't care for, public sentiment, for Wakefield folk were fond of their old market cross, and some were outraged at the very notion of its removal. Many of the country's provincial newspapers, some from far afield, such as *The Western Daily Press*, ran stories about how the sale had unfolded, most under the headline 'Strange scene at Wakefield'. The auction had been scheduled to take place in front of the market cross on Wednesday, 19 September 1866, and certain corporation officials were buoyed by the sight of so many people gathering to place their bids. But of course, that wasn't why they had come. It soon became clear, from the disquiet among the crowds, that this was a protest. Their anger was, in fact, vented at the wrong body, for it was the shopkeepers of Cross Square who had brought about the day's events. As one, they'd petitioned the corporation, insisting that the cross had had its day, having outgrown its original purpose. The corporation certainly weren't in universal agreement about this, for after the auctioneer, a Mr Dixon, had begun proceedings (by reading the particulars of sale from the sparsely produced handbill that advertised the auction), a Mr Councillor Burton stepped forward.

'Who authorized this sale, Mr Dixon?'

'Er, Mr Whitham, I believe.'

'The town clerk? Where is he? Is he here?'

Whitham couldn't be discerned, having wisely kept well clear of the town for the day.

'Mr Morgan,' Burton began again; 'is *he* here?'

Henry Morgan was the deputy town clerk, and hadn't expected the ambush. He made himself known to Burton, who turned his questions to him.

'Who gave Mr Whitham authority to instruct Mr Dixon to sell the market cross?' Burton demanded to know.

'I decline to answer the question,' came Morgan's reply.

'Decline to answer?' He then began to address the crowd as he warmed to his tune. 'Did you hear that, ladies and gentleman? Our market cross, which has stood since the days of Queen Anne, is about to be sold to the highest bidder, yet proper permission has not been given.' The crowd jeered and whistled. 'Ladies and gentleman, this sale is illegal!'

'Sir, really,' protested Mr Dixon, now mounted upon a soapbox by the steps of the cross. 'We must begin the auction.'

'How about a show of hands?' Burton suggested. 'This structure was built using money raised by public subscription, so it's only fair that the public decides its fate. Those in favour of its removal, raise your hands.'

Half a dozen onlookers duly put their hands in the air, looking around nervously as the eyes of the others were upon them.

'And those who wish to see the market cross remain?'

With a cheer, the rest of the crowd joined Councillor Burton by thrusting their arms aloft.

'Well, gentleman,' Burton said with a smile, turning to Mr Morgan and Mr Dixon; 'I think that concludes the matter. Not a shilling must be bid for that market cross.'

'Wait,' came a call from another official. It was Mr Bell, clerk to Mr Whitham, and he'd joined Mr Dixon on the soapbox. 'I have here the conditions of sale, which I shall proceed to read, so there can be no doubt of the legitimacy of this auction.'

But, according to the newspaper reports, no sooner had Mr Bell cleared his throat and started quoting from the convoluted text, then the crowd started 'yelling, hooting, and [making] other discordant noises'. One of the protestors shoved Mr Bell off the soapbox, causing Mr Dixon to lose his balance as well. But that was the limit of the violence, and a few minutes later, Mr Dixon, having given up on addressing the crowd, simply yelled 'bids please!'

Over the tumult he managed to make out a bid of £20. This was raised to £25, then to £30, before a final price of just £35 was agreed with Mr Thomas Armitage, of Saville Street. The auction was swiftly brought to an end, but not before Mr Craven, a Westgate plumber, had agreed to pay nineteen shillings and sixpence per hundredweight for the lead. Removal was to be immediate to avoid any further disturbances, and the bell, which stood at the summit of the cross, and had tolled earlier that day, fell silent forever.

Pillars from the cross eventually went to nearby Alverthorpe Hall, and for a time, one was situated in the grounds at the back of the former Art Gallery on Wentworth Terrace. Today, it is claimed that a pillar erected in the Secret Garden in Thornes Park is from the original market cross structure, though its size appears greatly reduced from those shown in the accompanying photographs, where a Victorian adult barely compares to a quarter of its height when stood upright against one of three front-facing pillars.

Affection for the market cross failed to diminish as the years passed, and curiously in 1938, as reported by the *Yorkshire Evening Post* on Friday, 30 September, an impressive replica of the market cross had been constructed. It was to be the showpiece for Ye Olde Market Fayre, arranged by the Wakefield Conservative Party, to be held at the Church Institute on Westgate on Wednesday, 5 October 1938. The article, sandwiched between talk of German advances towards Austria, and a meeting between Adolf Hitler, Benito Mussolini, Édouard Daladier and Neville Chamberlain (that would lead to the latter's 'peace in our

The bell from the old market cross, which predated the structure itself. *By courtesy of YAHS.*

Louisa Fennell's watercolour of the market cross at Cross Square, painted in 1900, long after it was taken down. *By courtesy of WLSL.*

Cross Square, drawn by Henry Clarke in the 1890s. *By courtesy of WLSL.*

time' declaration), described the intricacies of the replica model. It was made to a large scale by Ledgar Holdsworth, a town architect, complete with 'the old flower seller who will sit on the steps and sell her flowers'. On the day of the fair, the same paper reported that, along with the market cross, a replica of the front of the old Six Chimneys building on Kirkgate, and a model of the Shambles, which was an old street that connected Cross Square and the Bull Ring, were also on view. It would have proved a nostalgic day, when some of the oldest attendees might just about have recalled the time when the real market cross stood proudly in Cross Square.

Another relic of Wakefield's past was a cannon given to the town after the Siege of Sevastopol. The British Government arranged for major towns and cities across the Empire to receive these weapons, used by the Russians against them. Upon the Wakefield cannon, the following words were painted: 'Captured at Sebastopol, September 8th, 1855'.

Cross Square in 1884. *By courtesy of YAHS.*

Bull Ring and
Cross Square
in the twentieth
century.

To celebrate the passing through the town of the Leeds-bound Royal Train on 7 September 1858, the townsfolk had suspended flags from public buildings, including those on Wood Street, the parish church, the Corn Exchange and the House of Correction. According to the *Western Daily Press*, published the following day, 'crowds of well-dressed people' streamed towards 'the station of the Lancashire and Yorkshire Railway, which was the chief point of attraction … gaily decorated with a profusion of flags, and though some of these were not exactly appropriate to the occasion, they served to testify the loyalty of the parties contributing them.' The newspaper also reported that there were 'frequent discharges of cannon; the Sebastopol gun, lately presented to the town, being placed on the fair ground, where during the day it boomed forth in honour of the visit of Her Majesty to Yorkshire.'

Just a few months later, on 22 January 1859, the *Bury Times* reported the following:

Cross Square today showing Marmalade on the Square.

CURIOUS PRACTICAL JOKE IN WAKEFIELD

On Monday night, the inhabitants of Wakefield were alarmed by a loud report, subsequently found to have been caused by the discharge of the Russian gun lately presented to the town, which some mischievous person had loaded. Every pane was completely cleared out of one of the Court House windows; while other windows in the same and neighbouring building were smashed. The police have at present no clue to the perpetrators of this practical joke.

John Hewitt described this incident, calling the joker a 'mad-freak' who, at the time of the publication of his scarce volumes in the 1860s, remained at large. He recorded that many panes of glass were broken in the windows of the Music Saloon, and the nearby market cross, even

Shown in about 1880, this building, now used by Wakefield College, housed Wakefield Museum from 1955. It was previously the Institute of Literature and Science from 1910, and before that, from 1855, the Mechanics' Institution. It began life in the early 1820s as a music saloon, newsroom and library, with public baths also inside the building. *By courtesy of YAHS.*

suggesting that the discharge had caused the ground to shake. On 6 November 1858, the cannon had been 'placed within the Portico of the West-Riding Court House, Wood-street' and following the incident in January 1859, Hewitt wrote that the relic had been spiked, which he thought a sensible precaution, because the muzzle of the cannon had been 'pointing down Wood-street, at the bottom of which thoroughfare were numerous dwellings fronting the entrance to the wide street. Thus it is easy to perceive that if this cannon, in its present condition, were to be loaded with ball and fired off, the danger to property, life and limb would be great.'

It is perhaps thankful that cannon were not lying in Wood Street twenty-two years earlier, on Monday, 31 July 1837, when violent riots broke out during hustings for that year's general election. The election would see Whig candidate Lord Morpeth successfully contest the West Riding representation against the Tory, John Stuart-Wortley. Before the vote the candidates had attended Wakefield to give speeches, and on this occasion, when Lord Morpeth spoke about the recent Poor Law Amendment Act, the rioting, between the 'yellow' Whigs and 'blue' Tories, would prove fatal.

On 5 August, the *Leeds Intelligencer* printed a letter from one of its readers, B.H. Brook:

RIOT AT WAKEFIELD
'In the mouth of two or three witnesses the truth shall be established'

I WILL be as brief as possible: I went in at the Bottom of Wood-Street towards the Hustings at the Nomination at Wakefield, on Monday last, before the Business commenced, and when Lord Morpeth was saying that the Poor Law had met with more Opposition in the West-Riding of Yorkshire, than any other Part of the Nation, I left the Meeting to get some Refreshment. I went past the Court House down a back lane into Northgate, and entered a Public House, where a Blue Flag was hung out. I had not been in the Room above Ten or Fifteen Minutes, before a Gentleman with a Yellow-Favour, came in and told the Company what Disturbances were going on. He said he was sorry to say that it was begun or occasioned by a Band belonging to the Yellow Party, forcing their way up the Street amongst the Blues. This Gentleman had hardly related the Affair, before another Gentleman, with a Yellow Favour, came in and made a similar Statement. This Gentleman had but just sat down, when a third Gentleman, with a Yellow Favour, came in and told the Company the same story. After this Statement had been made by these Three Gentlemen, and each Statement made independent of the other, the Company present unanimously expressed their Approbation of the Honourable Conduct of those Three Gentlemen, for the very candid Manner in which they had expressed themselves against the Conduct of their own Party. All the Company present were strangers to me, but there was one Gentleman wearing a White Hat, who stated that Two of his Carriages had been damaged by Stones thrown at them as they were coming to Wakefield that Morning. I think this Gentleman was from Leeds; to him I appeal for the Truth of this Statement.

Yours respectfully, B.H. Brook
Huddersfield, 4 August 1837

Clearly, terrible trouble had broken out at the hustings, and the *Bradford Observer*, reporting on 3 August 1837, three days after the disturbance, summed up the events of that fateful Monday:

> It is utterly impossible to enumerate the broken heads and other severe wounds received by numerous persons during this lamentable riot. One gentleman (and while we regret his untimely fate, we cannot but feel thankful that it is only one) has died. The name of this unfortunate individual is Mr Carter of Ossett; he was struck on the head with a piece of the iron railing, which fractured his skull severely. He was taken to the Strafford Arms, and prompt medical assistance was rendered, but his wound was past the reach of skill. It was expected that an inquest would have been held on the body yesterday, but it was thought advisable to adjourn it till after the election; and it is therefore intended to hold it on Tuesday next. The deceased was among the crowd of Yellows in the Pit, when he received his death wound.

As it turned out, there would be further loss of life. A charwoman from Leeds named Margaret Moore also passed away as a result of the violence that broke out on Wood Street, when political fervour reached fever pitch. Margaret, a proud supporter of the Tories, was fond of attending the speeches that could be heard at these local hustings, always sporting in her cap a pretty blue rosette cut from ribbon when she did so. With a friend of hers, Elizabeth Sharp, who worked at Brown's flax mill on Mabgate in Leeds, she'd walked to Wakefield, eagerly anticipating the debates.

It was noon when they arrived on Wood Street, and the speeches were in full flow, but the pair soon realized something wasn't right. A mob had gathered, supposedly supporters of the Whigs, who'd arrived with a band of musicians, marching with them up Cross Square on to Wood Street, where insults were tossed about, the blues and yellows trading verbal blows.

Words soon turned to violence, and Elizabeth and Margaret tried to get away from the crowd as fighting broke out. They made it to the Music Saloon (lately Wakefield Museum, before Wakefield College took up the keys) just as bricks began to fly down the street. Elizabeth, scared for her life, squeezed past a couple of onlookers and found herself in a narrow street, without Margaret. She wouldn't see her again until she returned to Leeds, when she'd learn that her friend had been felled by a brick, and was stricken in Leeds Infirmary.

It seems that, just as Mr Brook had claimed in his letter to the *Leeds Intelligencer*, the violence began as Lord Morpeth had reached full flow on the subject of the Poor Law Amendment Act. Supporters of both parties fought with plain sticks, branches ripped from nearby trees, poles upon which they flew their colours, ever deadlier instruments. Bats, bricks and iron railings flew in all directions as heads were smashed open, and noses and lips were bloodied.

Contemporary newspaper reports, such as the *Lincolnshire Chronicle*, on 4 August 1837, stated that the blues, 'having been driven up an adjoining lane, appeared to have taken the opportunity of their temporary dispersion to arm themselves with bludgeons, and having formed themselves in order, again charged upon the orange party, and completely routed them.'

The Wood Street hustings had been erected beside a brick wall, which divided the street from a field in which the Whig supporters, many of whom had come from Huddersfield, had gathered in their thousands. More were fighting in the street, and when those being pursued by the Tory faithful ran to the field for safety, they knocked down part of the wall, sending bricks tumbling to the ground. These made perfect weapons when broken in two and used as brickbats. The blues had also got hold of bricks, and red missiles filled the air, thrown by protagonists whose aim was anything but true. More and more combatants appeared, swelling the ranks of both sides – some put the numbers at about 40,000 – and skirmishes were now raging at either end of Wood Street, by the cross, and in the market place. The hustings were abandoned as windows in the Tammy Hall, the Court House, and the Woodman Inn, within which yard the blues had retreated, were smashed to smithereens. It was Charles John Brandling, a West Riding magistrate, who read the

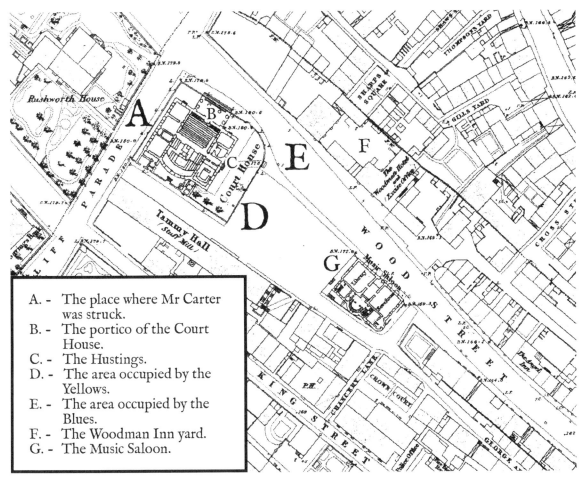

A. - The place where Mr Carter was struck.
B. - The portico of the Court House.
C. - The Hustings.
D. - The area occupied by the Yellows.
E. - The area occupied by the Blues.
F. - The Woodman Inn yard.
G. - The Music Saloon.

Plan of the riot showing the positions of the opposing parties. Reproduced using the 1851 1:1,056 OS Map of Wakefield and based on a crude plan used at the inquest into the death of Margaret Moore, which was published in the *Leeds Intelligencer* on 19 August 1837. *By courtesy of old-maps.co.uk, Ordnance Survey and Caroline Rochford.*

Riot Act, and the Dragoons were sent for to break up the trouble. By the time they arrived the rioters had fallen away, save for a few brawlers.

In the days that followed, as inquests into the deaths of Mr Carter and Ms Moore were held, it was determined that George Craven, for the Whigs, had given the signal for trouble to begin. It started when stick-carrying yellows had confronted their rivals, ripping out cards and emblems from the hats worn by the blues.

William Carter, the deceased, of Flushdyke Mill in Ossett, was a follower of the blues, and had worn his card and rosette on the day to show his support. After he was struck, by a boulder or a stone, he removed his hat, and as he staggered away, he was smashed over his bald head by a man armed with a staff. He was quickly conveyed to the Strafford Arms to receive medical assistance, as blood and vomit poured from his nostrils and his mouth. But despite the best efforts of a local surgeon, who bled poor Mr Carter to try to alleviate his torment, he died the following day.

Apparently a third person lost their life. The death of Mr John Maude, Esq., was lamented in *The Examiner* on 13 August 1837. He was described as a 'gentleman of large fortune, and a magistrate of the county, who was so desperately wounded by these ruffians, that he was obliged to be carried to the house of Mr Cassons, in Wood Street. During the night he vomited large quantities of blood, and in the morning he died in the greatest agony.'

On 30 December it was announced in the *Yorkshire Gazette* that subscriptions for William Carter's widow had been sent by 'the High Sheriff, the Earl of Harewood, Earl Fitzwilliam, Lord

TOWN HALL & COURT HOUSE, WAKEFIELD.

The Court House, shown in an old postcard, around which the riot took place.

Wharncliffe, Viscount Morpeth, Sir F.L. Wood, G.L. Fox, Esq. and several of the nobility and gentlemen connected with the West-Riding'.

The inquests held on the bodies of William Carter and Margaret Moore returned manslaughter verdicts against persons unknown in each instance.

Charges against persons known were brought, as reported by the *Leeds Intelligencer* on 5 August 1837. Aaron Sutcliffe was landlord of the King's Head, a public house on Kirkgate, and he was brought to the Court House on Wood Street charged with offences relating to the aftermath of the riot. According to solicitor John Marsden, clerk to the magistrates, soon after the military arrived to quell the trouble, following the reading of the Riot Act, he, Marsden, was stood in Wood Street, armed with a rather pathetic looking stick, fashioned from a thorn bush, with which he thought he might defend himself. It was to no avail, though, for poor Mr Marsden found himself on the wrong end of a couple kicks, delivered by a passing rioter, a navvy who'd joined in the trouble. It was then Mr Marsden spotted Sutcliffe, though at first he failed to recognize the publican. After Sutcliffe had grabbed Marsden's stick, the latter demanded to know the name of the former.

'If you are an Englishman, you will tell me your name.'

'Greenwood!' came the slurred reply, for the dishonest Sutcliffe had been sampling the produce of a local rival that afternoon.

At that point a woman walked past.

'Ey up, Aaron,' she called with a smile.

'Oh, I remember; it is Aaron Sutcliffe. You will lose your licence for this,' Marsden told him.

'I bloody won't,' spat Sutcliffe. 'Oi, Matty Dawson; come here and let this bugger have it.'

Matthew and George Dawson were brothers who lived at Storrs Hill, Ossett, and were known to Sutcliffe as they were regular frequenters of the King's Head. Matthew, or Matty, who along with George had been with Sutcliffe at the Angel in the town, answered the command and threw a bludgeon at Marsden, which only just missed the solicitor. It was then that the two brothers began walking menacingly towards Marsden, who now feared for his life. George tore off the lapel of the man's coat, and just before any blows could befall him, the woman who'd given Aaron's name away came back and stood between the men.

'Don't be so stupid, lads,' she said. 'Come on, let's go and find somewhere else to sup. And give that man his stick back.'

With that they left Mr Marsden unharmed.

The court found Sutcliffe guilty of common assault for taking the stick and fined him £1 8s. before warning him that when his licence was on the agenda at the next Brewster Sessions, the conviction would be taken into account.

As for the Dawson brothers, Matthew was ordered to pay £2 3s. and costs of 5s. for his part in a disturbance later that evening on Westgate Common when he assaulted three special constables, and again, as with Marsden, removed items of their clothing. George was formally reprimanded and dismissed.

A further charge was heard against a collier of Daw Green, named Squire Sykes. He'd been overheard boasting that he'd been involved in the smashing of windows at the Woodman Inn, expressing his joy that repairs had been carried out so swiftly, for it was his plan to smash them again another day. He was remanded in custody.

As it was, when the dust settled, Whig candidates Lord Morpeth and Sir George Strickland beat the Hon John Stuart-Wortley, and were duly elected to represent the West Riding at Parliament, though recriminations would continue well into the following year.

On 24 February 1838, the *Leeds Times* reported that John Briggs, the landlord of the said Woodman Inn, had sued the inhabitants of Agbrigg and Morley wapentake for damages to recover the costs of repairing the interior and exterior of his public house. He was allowed to sue the wapentake in the hope that the inhabitants might take collective responsibility for ensuring that in future, peace was better kept. It took the jury just twenty minutes to return a verdict in favour of Mr Briggs, and he was awarded £105.

It was earlier that year, on 10 January, when a notice appeared in the *Blackburn Standard*:

> On the 30th ult., at Ossett, the widow of the late Mr William Carter, was delivered of a daughter. The little stranger was born just five months after its lamented father was cruelly deprived of this life in the Wakefield election riots.

Not far from the scenes of the madding crowds, and some twenty-eight years later, Wakefield's Industrial and Fine Art Exhibition was held on 30 August 1865. Wakefield curate Reverend Charles Edward Camidge ran a night school for labouring men through the parish church and he thought it would be a capital idea to hold a small event at which his pupils might display some of their work. The idea grew, and all across the district, exhibitors keen to show off their skills to a wider audience, seized on the notion of a Yorkshire exhibition to rival those regularly held in London.

Such was the level of interest that a special building, the Central Hall, was erected near the Court House to accommodate the exhibition, and according to the *York Herald*, on 2 September 1865, the exhibition was opened amid much pomp and ceremony. The newspaper described the building as

Wood Street in 1885. *By courtesy of YAHS.*

Wood Street today.

a temporary wooden structure occupying land adjacent to the recently vacated Tammy Hall on Wood Street, which also housed part of the event. The committee set up to oversee proceedings had provided 17,500 square feet of table and floor space, and as a result, 1,400 exhibitors were in attendance. There was some pressure for the event to prove a success, for the erection of the building, designed by local architect William Watson, and built by Messrs Latham, had cost upwards of £700. The paper described the building as follows:

It covers a rectangular site, and comprises an entrance vestibule flanked by picture galleries, and communicating directly with a large central hall, through which access is gained to the rooms of the Tammy Hall. On each side of the entrance and opening into the central hall, is a picture gallery, both of which may be considered models of what rooms should be. They are 50 feet long, their width is 30, and their height is 20 feet. They are airy and commodious, and they are admirably lighted from raised rectangular windows in the roof. Of the two apartments the north contains the finest collection, and is given up entirely to paintings in oils. The walls of the other are hung with the remainder of such works placed at the disposal of the committee, and with an excellent collection of water colours, photographs, chromo-lithographs, and drawings. There are in all upwards of 670 works of art, of which about 220 are shown in the north gallery. It would be impossible in a brief notice to do justice to the high merit of either collection, and it is sufficient at present to say that they have been contributed by some of the greatest collectors in the West Riding, that there are among them many pictures of the highest class, and almost entirely of the English school, and that there are very few indeed which do these any discredit by being associated with them.

On display, according to Camidge's own *A History of Wakefield and its Industrial and Fine Art Exhibition*, which was published the following year, were paintings by the likes of Hogarth, Gainsborough, Reynolds, Constable, Turner, and several others.

The York newspaper also gave a description of the industrial element of the exhibition, which it termed the most important department of the event. This was, the report described, held chiefly in the Tammy Hall and was entered via steps leading from the central hall.

Wakefield Fine Art Exhibition, from the *Leeds Mercury*.

It consists of two narrow but very long rooms, the lower of which is provided with shafting, and has therefore been assigned to machinery in motion, and the upper of which, a very fine apartment originally used for the exhibition of woollen goods, is fitted up with an immense variety of specimens of our manufacturers, contributed by a still larger number of exhibitors.

The Tammy Hall had officially opened on Friday, 10 July 1778 to sell Worsted material. The *Leeds Intelligencer* stated that the occasion was celebrated by the 'ringing of bells, and every other demonstration of joy; a great Number of Cloth Merchants, &c. attended, and upwards of one thousand Pieces of Tammy were brought up; besides quantities of White Broadcloth, Blankets &c. &c.' In 1870 the building was partially demolished to make way for a new town hall. The part of the building that survived became a police station in 1878, its grand opening taking place on 24 October that year. The police station was equipped with a tunnel that led from the cells, of which there were nineteen, to the borough court in the newly opened Town Hall. A carving of a policeman wearing his helmet can still be seen on the wall of the old station, facing on to Cliff

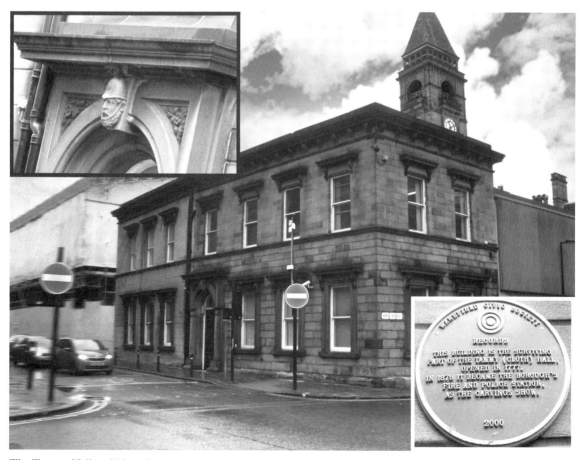

The Tammy Hall and blue plaque.

Parade. In recent years, the building has been the home of Wakefield and Pontefract Magistrates' Court, the closure of which was announced in 2016.

Back at the exhibition of 1865, there were eleven sections in the industrial department for visitors to observe. These were:

1. Chemical products and manufacturers, and mineral substances
2. Glass, china, and earthenware
3. Furniture, wood work, house decoration, fancy work etc.
4. Carpeting, woollen fabrics, woolwork etc.
5. Machinery, tools, ironmongery, and metal work
6. Models
7. Philosophical and musical instruments
8. Carriages and harnesses
9. Clothing
10. Stationery, printing, bookbinding, penmanship, etc.
11. Scholars' and children's work.

A section where drawings, paintings and sculptures could be seen was also available and it was said in total, across all the sections, that there were more than 700 items on display.

The opening day, Wednesday, 30 August 1865, was an auspicious occasion and another when Wakefield's inhabitants came out in their hundreds, perhaps thousands, to support the cause. The days immediately preceding that Wednesday had been wet and gloomy, and there were fears that a washout might convince people to stay indoors, but the good weather returned and sunshine heralded the splendour that awaited. House after house was decorated proudly with flags of bright and bold colours, and those who didn't fancy being bounced along in the thronged streets below cheered and waved from their windows. Others packed into the churchyard on Kirkgate watching a procession that included policemen, the orders of Oddfellows and Foresters, local gentry, West Riding Magistrates, the mayor and the Corporation, the architect and the contractors, the committee, the president in his open carriage with the Archbishop of York, and the clergy, all accompanied by a band of musicians.

The president was Lord Houghton, that is to say, the poet and politician Richard Monckton Milnes, son of the late Robert Pemberton Milnes and Henrietta Maria, Vicountess Galway. He was expected to arrive in the town early in the afternoon on the London train, but it was delayed, to the concern of those waiting for him in the streets. When Lord Houghton finally arrived, he was cheered on by the gathered masses. At fifteen minutes past three the procession reached the Tammy Hall and was led into the building, where inside, a Mr Emerson played the organ, accompanied by an orchestra and a choir 2,000 voices strong, who sang the *Old Hundredth Psalm*, after which one of the guests of honour, the Archbishop of York, read a prayer. Lord Houghton followed this with an address in which he spoke of his wish that those attending would enjoy themselves and that such an event was a national act of justice that honoured the English artisans who'd lived in austerity while they created their great works, now exhibited in fine buildings fit to house them. He continued:

> It was no small consideration, that art which used to be confined to a few persons – which used to be the mere appendage of the rich and the powerful – were now becoming necessarily considered as the due heritage of the mass of the community. They might be thankful indeed that they had lived to see their picture galleries and collections of art and interest, kept not closed up … but generally open throughout the country for the public culture of the great people of England.

Lord Houghton urged employers of labouring men to allow their employees leave to come to visit the exhibition, for he felt that this would be beneficial to both parties: the employee returning to work with a sense of satisfaction, and their minds 'much opened and improved'. He cautioned his listeners to try to ensure that, in his spare time, the working man was engaged with something other than the mechanical labour in which they were otherwise employed. For man must not feel that 'he was part of a mere machine' but part of the 'great machine of the world', because 'there was something divine in him [man] which gives him the power of understanding and appreciating other things besides mechanical works, thus placing him in conjunction and sympathy with minds higher than his own.' And with that he wished the exhibition every success, a sentiment met with loud cheers.

Lord Houghton's wish was granted, reviews declaring the event a triumph; the *Leeds Intelligencer*, on 9 September 1865, writing that 'all persons who visited this exhibition speak of it in terms of almost unqualified praise. A finer collection of the works of art, combined with those of industry, has never been seen in Yorkshire, and both the promoters and the contributors may feel gratified with the result of their labours.'

Attendance was healthy, with 2,010 visitors paying sixpence each at the turnstiles on Saturday, 2 September, and a further 750 colliers from Messrs Thorp's North Gawber and Willow Bank Collieries attending at the expense of their employers, who also footed the colliers' rail fares, clearly paying heed to Lord Houghton's words of advice. Numbers swelled, with 2,738 paying sixpence the following Monday and 1,146 having paid for a season ticket. And the newspaper reckoned that there was talk of from 4,000 to 6,000 visitors attending the following Saturday alone via the Lancashire and Yorkshire railway line. Applications to visit the exhibition poured in from factories, mills, coal mines and headmasters of schools, all desperate to allow their employees and pupils a glimpse at the displays on offer. And it wasn't just industry and art that entertained all the visitors. In addition to the organ recitals and the choir, the band of the Rifle Corps offered to play, and on Tuesday, 5 September the band of the West Riding Pauper Lunatic Asylum accompanied the resident orchestra, a band described by the newspaper as 'an excellent one'. On the Thursday, the members of the Glee and Madrigal Society gave their songs and glees, and then on 8 September, the 2nd West York Militia Band, based in York, whose commanding officer was Colonel Smyth, gave their own concert.

Proceedings were finally brought to a close on 19 October following a ceremony described in several provincial newspapers. It was reckoned that about 180,000 people visited the exhibition during the six weeks that it was held. The weather, for the most part, remained good, and the inhabitants of the town continued to fly their flags, as one paper had put it, as if there was a 'constant holiday'. The *Sheffield Daily Telegraph*, reporting the day after the close of the event, reckoned that in the first week, 18,510 visitors attended, increasing to 24,079 in the second week, 30,310 in week three, 33,163 in the fourth week, that figure rising to 38,190 and decreasing, in the final week, to 34,456. When the event's finance secretary, William Stott Banks, the local author, who won one of the exhibition's second class certificates for his *Provincial Words in Use at Wakefield*, produced the final accounts, it was shown that the exhibition had made a healthy profit of over £3,000, which was put towards funding Wakefield's inaugural school of art.

The closing ceremony, coming on 19 October 1865, fell a day after the Prime Minister, Henry John Temple, 3rd Viscount Palmerston, died in office, and as Lord Houghton gave his closing remarks he acknowledged the tragedy of the previous day:

> In the great historic event which yesterday darkened the surface of English life, we recognize that He who gives is also He who taketh away – we recognize that in this world we build up buildings that are taken down in tears; we raise up hopes, and those hopes vanish; we cultivate the highest virtues and talents, and death carries them away.

He thanked everybody present for attending the exhibition and wished that they would do all in their power to promote similar institutions as the Wakefield Industrial and Fine Art Exhibition 'by which advantages may be given to the lower classes of the community which have hitherto been enjoyed mainly by the higher, by which all classes of people in this country may be bound and welded together so as to promote the common interest and the common prosperity.' Before a grand concert raised the spirits of the assembled, and at its conclusion carried them away with happy hearts, William Henry Leatham, the then Liberal MP for Wakefield, and a native of the town, told those gathered that he hoped the music would lift the gloom cast over 'the most beautiful spectacle that ever adorned the town of Wakefield'.

An entirely different spectacle would have been cast by the dropping well that, according to Hewitt, once stood at the bottom of Chestnut Close, on the east side of lower Northgate. The College public house was formerly named the Chestnut Inn, and the close was situated at the end of Chestnut Lane, the start of which was the site of modern-day Howard Street.

The chestnut trees honoured by the names of the close and the lane stood in a field (the close) comprising 6 acres that hosted games of football and cricket. This area gradually developed during the nineteenth century as the need for housing increased. Hewitt stated that there were fourteen or fifteen trees in total, all of which were felled during the said century, as the housing estates took their place. The well he spoke of can perhaps be seen in the image overleaf, which is an Ordnance Survey map from 1851, showing the site of a 'D. Well' behind a sandstone quarry.

By 1864, the year he produced one of the volumes of his book on Wakefield's history, Hewitt claimed there was just one tree still standing, the others having been felled from 1858 onwards. He recalled that the branches of the trees reached halfway over Northgate, 'and formed a very good shelter in rainy or stormy weather, as well as a cool and refreshing shade in sultry or warm summer seasons.' When the last remaining trees were removed, and the houses erected, a former sandstone quarry, visible on the map, was also covered. 'There was in this quarry,' Hewitt explained, 'a spring of water, from which ran many small streams down the sides of the rock, a fall of some 20 feet or more; and these dropping streams much resembled the Dropping Well at Knaresborough.'

The inhabitants of the town used to visit the spring with tin cans and other vessels, and carry water back to their homes for domestic use. Hewitt remembered that it was soft water, of an 'excellent' quality, and if only it had been collected into a reservoir and 'brought in pipes to the dwellings of the inhabitants, it would have been both a good, and an excellent supply of water for household uses.' It being too late for anything to be done about any of this, he concluded, with an air of sadness, 'Wakefield has lost many natural advantages, and the loss of this supply of water may be instanced as one of the many opportunities which this town has let slip from it.'

Though Hewitt wrote fondly of the close, and the pleasurable pastimes enjoyed therein, he did not lament its loss too greatly for he felt the improvements to the town that the houses erected

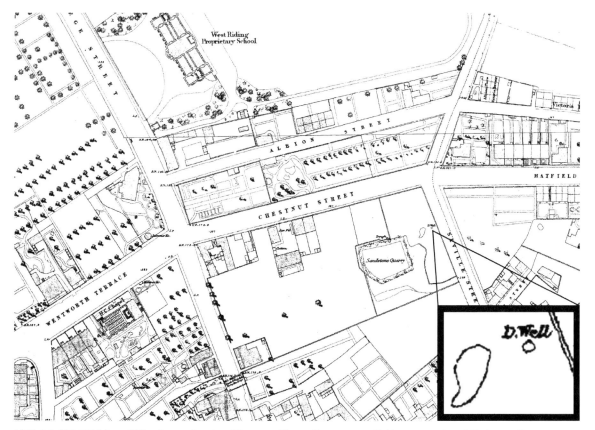

1851 1:1,056 OS Map of Northgate showing Chestnut Close. *By courtesy of old-maps.co.uk and Ordnance Survey.*

The College public house.

upon it had brought were as good as any in Wakefield. But ever the poet, he did pen these few lines of verse:

> *In early life I've gambolled in,*
> *Old merry Wakefield's Chestnut Close,*
> *And tasted pleasures free from sin,*
> *When Sol went down and when he rose.*
> *But other times have come to me,*
> *Long years have rolled and passed away;*
> *The Chestnut Trees nowhere I see,*
> *And other scenes now rule the day.*

A scene that John Hewitt would not live to see (he died in Ossett in 1890) was the unveiling of the statue of Queen Victoria, on 15 February 1905, the same day the foundation stone was laid of the recently extinct free library on Drury Lane. Though the statue would be removed to various sites, its original (and subsequent) home was the Bull Ring, where it would stand for forty-five

Mother Shipton's dropping well.

years, before a thirty-five-year spell in Clarence Park saw the much-loved depiction of indomitable majesty return to the Bull Ring in 1985, only to be replaced, nearly twenty-five years later, by a fountain. On Wednesday, 28 October 2009, Councillor Denise Jeffery oversaw the removal of the statue to a new home in Castrop Rauxel Square, where it stands guard before the multi-storey car park on Rishworth Street. Back in February 1905, the unveiling proved a grand affair, and excitement had been building in the town as the day approached. On 7 February, with just over a week to go, the *Yorkshire Post and Leeds Intelligencer* announced:

COMING EVENTS AT WAKEFIELD

The Mayoress of Wakefield (Mrs Childe) will on the 15th instant unveil a handsome bronze statue of Queen Victoria, which has been subscribed by the citizens and erected upon a suitable pedestal of polished Peterhead granite in the Bull Ring. Subsequently the Mayor (Councillor H.S. Childe) will lay the foundation stone of the Carnegie Free Library, which is being erected in Drury Lane, and to the cost of which Mr Carnegie is contributing £8,000. These interesting functions will be followed by a Mayoral reception in the town Hall.

The following Wednesday, the day arrived, described by the same paper as a 'memorable day in Wakefield'.

'In its long life,' the article began, 'Wakefield has seen many memorable sights. Few however, will deserve a worthier place in its history than the demonstration that took place yesterday afternoon.' It went on to explain that the subscription had raised £1,000, and this was the total cost of the statue. The newspaper described it thus:

[It is] of bronze, and stands 10 feet in height, wearing robes of semi-State, with skirt of Honiton lace, while on the head rests a small diamond crown, from beneath which falls a long veil of Honiton lace, the lines of which are continued by stately folds of a silken train. The ornaments are bracelets, brooch, and necklace of diamonds, the decorations being the Order of Victoria and Albert, and of the Crown of India, in addition to the Ribbon of the Garter with badge and star. The upper part of the plinth bears a tracing of Indian design, which serves a double purpose – assisting to modify the sudden transition from a costume so replete with minute ornaments to the bare, smooth surface of the base, and possessing a certain symbolic significance of the great Eastern Empire over which the Queen held sway.

Unveiling of the Queen Victoria Statue in 1905.

A crowd of dignitaries had assembled from the neighbouring areas of Dewsbury, Barnsley, Brighouse, Morley, Batley and Ossett. Also present were the town clerk, the vicar of Wakefield, members of the corporation, and the honourable secretary of the Memorial Committee. And at the very moment the statue was unveiled, the band of the King's Own Yorkshire Light Infantry burst into tune, treating those gathered to a rendition of the National Anthem. The late Queen's son, King Edward, even sent a telegraph praising the 'loyal feeling which induced the inhabitants of Wakefield to erect a statue in memory of the late Queen'.

One elderly citizen present, Henry Smith, recalled when the Queen, then a princess, had visited Wakefield in 1830. It's likely he was actually remembering Victoria's only visit to the town, made with her mother, the Duchess of Kent, in September 1835, when the pair travelled through Wakefield towards Wentworth Woodhouse. As they made their way to their destination (having earlier departed Harewood House), escorted by the Wakefield troop of the Yeomanry Cavalry, the young princess was startled by the strange, unwelcome sight of a blue hand, which was thrust suddenly into her carriage. It belonged to one of the workers at the nearby Belle Isle Dyeworks, and overcome by the excitement of the occasion, he'd approached the carriage without giving his gesture much thought. It certainly upset the 15-year-old princess, and she was taken to Mrs Hargrave's Sandal Hall, off Barnsley Road, where she was able to compose herself before her journey resumed.

Belle Isle Dyeworks, drawn by Henry Clarke. *By courtesy of WLSL.*

The statue has not been without controversy, notwithstanding public outcry on the occasions it has been moved. On 31 March 1908, John William Wrightson, of Queen Street, while in the employ of the Wakefield Window Cleaning Company, had an unfortunate mishap as he cleaned the new statue. As he was going about his duties, the ladder he was standing upon cracked and broke, sending poor Wrightson hurtling to the ground where he sustained chest and wrist injuries. He was taken to Clayton Hospital, where he was detained.

On 3 February 1936, the curious headline of 'Statue Baiting' appeared in the *Yorkshire Post*, with the following story published underneath:

Public statues are receiving unceremonious treatment these days. The latest outbreak of statue baiting I see is in the Bull Ring at Wakefield. Controversy has broken out – as our news columns have already borne witness – over the Victoria statue there, which it is suggested, is a source of trouble to traffic.

But Wakefield people should take note of what happened in Sheffield before they moved the only public statue in the town.

Sandal Hall, off Barnsley Road, drawn by Henry Clarke. *By courtesy of WLSL.*

Sandal Hall today.

The writer proceeded to explain that the Sheffield statue, also depicting Queen Victoria, which stood on an island, had been removed to a public park (just as would be the case in 1950 in Wakefield). However, the traffic problem only worsened after this. The newspaper had already reported on the 'future of a statue at Wakefield' on 31 January 1936. It was stated then that the city was embarking upon a new road scheme at a cost of £2 million and the statue, not yet a quarter of a century old, was in the way of the ambitious plans. The article said that even at the time of its erection in 1905, its location had been a cause for debate because it was felt that not enough room had been left between tram lines. In January 1936, it was suggested that the statue be removed to the bridge over the river Calder, newly opened at the time, and the public park was also mooted (a site that eventually provided a home to the statue). As it was, the statue was left in place, and actually aided traffic congestion, acting as a natural barrier. However, public opinion was strongly behind its removal to the park. But just over a year later, as preparations were being made for the town's celebration of the coronation of King George VI and Queen Elizabeth, on 12 May 1937, further trouble broke out. Five days before the coronation, word spread that plans had been made to completely cover the statue by boarding it up for the duration of the celebrations. 'Disloyal' were the cries of the public, who felt that their statue should not be hidden away on a royal occasion such as a coronation. An architect named W. Harold Watson was interviewed by the *Yorkshire Post* and he declared it 'an insult to His Majesty to box up his great grandmother at the time of the coronation'. He did not hold his tongue when he added:

> The statue is a masterpiece by one of the greatest sculptors of the age, and is one of the finest, if not the finest, statues of Queen Victoria in the country. If those responsible had taken their decorations to the top of her pedestal by 'stepping' their garden up to her feet and then had the statue cleaned, and perhaps floodlighted, it would have been a very fine show and a graceful act of respect to the greatest Queen this Empire has ever known.

These were indeed strong words in support of leaving the Queen just so. But the then Provost of Wakefield, the Very Reverend Noel Hopkins, though sensitive to the locals' feelings on the matter, thought the architect's words were misguided.

> Much as some people deplore the Victorian age and its enormities, it seems rather a shame that they should show their displeasure by wreaking vengeance upon the figure of the Queen, who after all, although responsible for many of its conventions, nevertheless, acted in good faith and did her best. The statues of Beaconsfield and others in London are being covered I understand, and if those who served her so faithfully are to be so treated I do not see that the Queen herself has any ground for complaint. I do not deplore the covering of the statue, but I do deplore covering up in such a way that gives it the appearance of a nesting hen. Apart from that I see no ground for complaint.

But this wasn't the end of the matter. On 10 May, just two days before the big day, a 'deputation of citizens' armed themselves with a petition and went off in search of the mayor, George Hemingway. Their petition, without wasting words, demanded the removal of the boarding, which had, by then, been erected. Mr Hemingway gave the petitioners a sympathetic ear, but told them their protestations were in vain. Plans had been made and carried out, and nothing could be changed at this late hour. Their last throw of the dice had not achieved the outcome they had hoped for, and it was decided not to press Mr Hemingway further. And now, almost eighty years later, with Queen Victoria approaching a decade spent in her new home in Castrop Rauxel Square, the public might wonder when she might be moved again, and to where.

The crowds of 15 February 1905 were almost matched in number by those who came out on Saturday, 6 October 1827 on Wood Street to see Mr Charles Brown, the famous aeronaut, ascend in his great balloon. Charles Brown had been active for the past few years, providing spectacular scenes in the skies above many provincial towns and cities across the country, and Wakefield had been abuzz with excitement ever since posters began to appear announcing the forthcoming ascent. A similar poster from a few years earlier, advertising an event in Sheffield, had read:

The Queen Victoria Statue today.

AEROSTATION
MR C. BROWN,
The Aeronaut
Begs leave most respectfully to inform the Gentry and Public in general, that he has just completed a most magnificent

BALLOON
(In which he intends shortly to ascend,) which will be exhibited (THIS DAY), July 17, 1824, and every Day, (Sundays excepted,) until further Notice in a Building erected for that purpose in Carver Street.

In the construction of this splendid Machine and its Appendages, neither labour nor expense have been spared. The dimensions of the Balloon are 35 feet diameter – is formed of gores of Silk 33 inches wide, and upwards of 60 feet long, in alternate colours of Crimson and White, manufactured in a peculiar manner, solely for the purpose. The Balloon is divided, from the Equator upwards, by then horizontal bands of silk, intersecting and forming a double at every joint, which adds considerably to the Balloon against expansion; it is again divided by forty-eight perpendicular bands, so that it forms an interior net, which adds considerable strength to the whole surface.

Mr B. has so contrived, that he has it in his power to ascend in ten minutes after the Gas is introduced into Balloon.

To the Balloon is attached

A SPLENDID CAR

Covered and beautifully ornamented, and lined with rich Crimson Silk.

Over the Car is suspended a beautiful festooned

CANOPY

N.B. The whole of the Balloon and its Appendages have been constructed by Mr C. Brown

☞ Doors will be open for Exhibition, from Nine o' Clock in the Morning, until Nine in the Evening.

Admission Tickets, – Ladies and Gentleman, 2s. each. Working People, 1s. Families consisting of Four Persons or more, 1s. 6d. each.

Tickets to be had at the INDEPENDENT, IRIS, and MERCURY officers; and at the Door of the Exhibition.

A planned ascent over Barnsley in September of the same year had ended in near peril when the weather forced the aeronaut into an abrupt landing. A large crowd had gathered close to a parcel of ground near a gas works, and Brown arrived, according to the *Sheffield Independent*, in 'excellent spirits'. The balloon rose without problems, and Brown reported seeing Pontefract quite clearly, but he then became lost in dark and dense clouds, throwing out ballast to try to land safely, as the balloon span around, tossed about by strong winds. He finally landed in Burton Salmon, near Ferrybridge, where a chaise boy, who'd been watching the descent, arranged for transport to take Mr Brown back to Barnsley.

He then promised to make what was to be his fourth ascent over Wakefield. True to his word, notices were placed in local newspapers, and on 11 September 1824, the following appeared in the *Sheffield Independent*:

BALLOON

The Public are respectfully informed, that it is the intention of MR CHAS. BROWN, of Sheffield, (who made his successful Ascent from Barnsley, on Tuesday last,) to ASCEND from WAKEFIELD, in his most Splendid Balloon, during the approaching Festival, being his Fourth Ascent.

Wakefield, Sept 9, 1824.

A few weeks after this advert was placed, the ballooning world lost one of its number when William Wyndham Sadler died aged just thirty, while making his thirty-first ascension. He rose above Bolton on 29 September, but after securing his grappling hook to a tree mid-flight, and attempting to land, he fell victim to a sudden gust of wind that snapped the rope holding the hook in place. This sent the balloon back towards the skies, until the car collided with the chimney stack of a tin-plate worker's shop. Sadler was thrown out of the car upon collision. As he fell, his feet got caught in the netting and he floated towards the ground, still attached to the netting, his terrifying journey covering a distance of about 2 miles. Just 20 yards from safety, he came loose, landing in a field. He fractured his skull upon impact, and though he lingered for a few hours, surgery being attempted during this time, he died the following morning. His travelling companion had been rendered unconscious when the balloon hit the chimney, and when he came round he was shocked to his core to learn he was alone in the car, but he bravely brought the balloon down, hitting a fence a mile from Whalley, in Lancashire, as he made his landing. Though he broke his arm, he walked away relatively unscathed; but the dangers of aeronautics had been laid bare for all to see.

This didn't stop Charles Brown, who made another ascent over Sheffield in August 1825, the newspapers of the day describing the affair as being generally successful, though not without complications. Hyde Park, which at the time was being readied to become a new cricket ground for Sheffield Cricket Club, and later became home to an enormous block of flats, was the chosen venue for the launch. Eventually Brown was seen floating over the town.

He attempted to repeat the excursion, accompanied by his younger brother, Roger, once more in 1827, just weeks before the forthcoming Wakefield spectacle of July that year. During preparations for the Sheffield voyage, to be made in a balloon named *Herschell*, the Brown brothers, seated within their car, suddenly found a small hole at the bottom of the balloon, out of which gas was escaping. Some spectators thought this had been planned, that the aeronauts wanted an excuse not to ascend, and duly left the park, booing and grumbling as they exited. Desperate not to disappoint those who'd remained, Charles Brown made a rudimentary repair of the tear, and the brothers began to rise above the ground, as applause drowned out the gasps of concern. But no sooner had the balloon begun its ascent than the tear in the material appeared again, 'large enough', explained the *Sheffield Independent*, 'to reveal to the eye a large portion of the interior of the balloon.' Despite the obvious danger this presented, the air remained calm, and the Brown brothers 'continued their course for little more than an hour, when they effected a safe descent at Brampton, near Chesterfield,' and on returning to Sheffield received a 'hearty welcome' from those gathered at the King's Head public house to receive them. No doubt many a spectator breathed a sigh of relief when word of the safe landing reached them. In fact, there were upwards of 12,000 people inside the park, and it was reckoned by the newspaper that the same number again lined the streets. No wonder, then, so many people turned out in Wakefield that October to see another feat of aeronautics. And if Charles Brown could successfully navigate a balloon with a great big hole in it, then what could possibly go wrong?

The ascent was to take place at around three in the afternoon on Saturday, 6 October 1827, and a great throng of people had arrived on Wood Street, where they gathered outside the door of the Woodman Inn, opposite which was a 'vacant piece of ground', according to several newspapers reporting from the scene. It was from this patch of land that the balloon was to take off. Curious members of the Wakefield public had heard all about the amazing feats achieved by Charles Brown, not least of his recent ascent in a gaping balloon and, his popularity increasing, they weren't to be denied the chance to see his vehicle take to the skies.

However, unbeknown to the spectators, Mr Brown had taken ill on the Friday evening, and was described by the *Wakefield and Halifax Journal* on 12 October 1827 as being 'indisposed'. There was no chance of him ascending, for he couldn't muster the strength to leave his bed. But, as the paper stated, 'that the public might receive no disappointment, an express was sent to Sheffield for a younger brother, who with a laudable readiness, immediately obeyed the call, and arrived in Wakefield on Saturday morning, a little after six o' clock.' It was time for Roger to take centre stage.

All of this meant that arrangements were delayed. The inflation of the balloon began four hours later than planned. And as the appointed hour approached and there was no sign of an aeronaut, the crowd became rather restless, or as the newspaper put it, 'symptoms of uneasiness and discontent began to manifest themselves.' Had the jitters and catcalls not abated, the assembly might not have heard the announcement explaining that Roger Brown had agreed to step into the breech and fly his older brother's balloon solo – something he'd hitherto not attempted. The spectators were asked to return just before half-past five when the necessary inflation would be complete, and Roger would be ready to board the car and give them a show to remember.

With the balloon eventually filled with as much gas as could be spared in order that the ascent might take place at the new time, Roger entered the car. The balloon's gas chamber not being at full capacity meant that any additional weight that could be spared had to be left on the ground – consequently, the grappling hooks were left behind. Roger smiled, not too convincingly, and waved a flag at the crowd, as a cry of 'Let go!' went up. A reporter despatched to Wakefield by the *Leeds Patriot* described how the balloon 'rose majestically, and soared steadily to the clouds in a westerly direction, and entered them in about five minutes.' This caused whoops of joy from those watching below, eager to spot the emergence of Roger and the balloon.

But when it was spotted again, joy turned to concern, for the balloon was suddenly heading straight back to the ground. It was seen to be moving rapidly earthwards with Roger apparently no longer in control, and 'the balloon seemed to have collapsed.' It was as if all the air had come gushing out, the limp canvas no longer enabling a smooth journey through the air. And not only that, Roger was all too aware of his perilous situation and his cries of help, and other terrified shrieks, confirmed the worst fears of the spectators. The flight had gone horribly wrong, and no mistake. Memories of Sadler's demise must have come flooding back to those in the know, and the crowds surely expected that the Fates had the same horrible end in store for Roger Brown. But there were no tin-workers' chimney stacks in the way this time, and the deflated balloon just kept on travelling westward in the direction of Flanshaw, where some of the spectators, guessing its course, had left in pursuit of the balloon and its unfortunate occupant.

It was close to this little village where Roger Brown finally crash-landed. Those first on the scene witnessed the prostrate figure being dragged out of his car by two young boys who'd been passing in their pony-driven gig. Roger's life had been spared, though he was insensible. The boys, with the help of some of the arriving spectators, lifted Roger into the gig and he was conveyed to the house of a Wakefield surgeon, Mr Bennet, who was able to declare that the stand-in aeronaut was relatively unharmed, though he had fractured an ankle and a fibula, painful souvenirs of his exploits.

When he was well enough to relay what had happened above the streets of Wakefield, Roger Brown explained that almost as soon as he'd entered the clouds, 'the balloon and car became violently agitated' and he found it quite unmanageable to navigate as a burst of wind, which Roger described as more like a hurricane, threatened to blow him out of the sky. Unsure what to do, and without his experienced elder brother to take the reins, Roger, who by this point had been dislodged from his little seat, took what he hoped was decisive action. Seeing a rope dangling invitingly before him, he reached out and took hold of it, seizing it with all his might. Unfortunately for young Roger, he'd grabbed hold of the very rope that controlled the supply of gas to the balloon, and by pulling it he'd performed the action designed to allow the gas to escape by way of releasing

Looking down Flanshaw Road, from Batley Road.

a safety valve. The gas poured out so swiftly that by the time the gravitas of what he'd done had dawned on him, and he'd let go of the rope, there was only a tiny amount of gas remaining, and without the buoyancy required to stay afloat, Roger began plummeting towards Flanshaw.

But this didn't stop Charles Brown, and the newspapers were soon full of accounts of his further exploits over the skies of England.

Chapter Three

Kirkgate

One of the main attractions drawing the members of the Huddersfield Archaeological and Topographical Society to Wakefield on that summer's day in August 1869 was the building known colloquially as the Six Chimneys. Walker described the three-storey structure, its architect unknown, in simple terms when he said: 'The Six Chimneys is the finest old house still standing in the town, and was built soon after Queen Elizabeth came to the throne.' His vivid description, which followed, resonates with surviving images, outliving the building itself, which fell to the ground in 1941 due to bodged improvements attempted by its owner, amid a campaign by the council to tear it down. Wakefield's once prized possession is commemorated today in name only by the J.D. Wetherspoon's public house on Kirkgate.

In Walker's day, he saw a part-brick, part-oak built building, a portion of which bore the date 1566 on 'the tie-beam of the southern gable', which he said was 'also carved upon what was originally the main entrance to the house on the eastern or garden side, the front of the building.' He also noted that the tie-beam of the central gable showed a hunting scene, where a hound was depicted pursuing a stag. Carvings of hunters in their tunics and in possession of weapons was depicted standing on corbels, jutting out of the walls. Outside there were stables and a fine garden, through which, Walker told his readers, 'flowed the Skitterick, on its way towards the river.'

For those visiting when the Topographical Society came to town, the building was one of 'the many quaint old houses which the town, a few years back contained'. In their time it was described in the report of their excursion as 'almost the last remaining', and as:

> the venerable palatial structure … which still affords a specimen of our ancient domestic architecture, and as the beholder gazes on its curious carvings and overhanging stories, the imagination, again peopling the house with olden inhabitants, wanders back to the 'good old times', 300 years ago, when notwithstanding the terrible and disastrous ordeal through which the town had passed during the recent civil war, its thriving townsfolk proved such gleesome company as to earn for it for the cheerful cognomen of 'Merrie Wakefield'.

Halfway through their Wakefield visit, and just before taking lunch, the members of the society arrived at the Six Chimneys, and were taken to the back of the building, which was formerly the front. As they'd made their way through the town, interested bystanders had joined their party, and by the time the gathering congregated to listen to Mr Fennell, of the society, give his paper on the building, their ranks had swelled considerably.

He began his pre-lunch talk by stating that no documents of authenticity had been found regarding the old history of the house, and that the building itself 'must be its own historian to us of the present day.' Fennell told his keen listeners that the frontage of the building, with its particular structure and ornamental oaken figures, made it quite clear that it dated back to the time of Henry VIII, or his daughter, Elizabeth I. A chimney sweep had assured Mr Fennell that the chimney top allowed easy descent to the basement, 'if any were inclined to take that downward course.' In that basement stood a great fireplace, which was '16 feet from tree to tree, indicative of good hospitality to many a guest and retainer'. The guests would enter via what was called the carriageway; this was either side of the grand entrance, where intricately carved wooden figures lined the route. The building was famed for its carved figures of bearded men in tunics and girdles, one carrying a spear, another with a hatchet resting over his shoulder, an axe wielded in his other hand. Another figure, 'situate to the left of the grand porch of old days', held a baton, and had his right hand held to his mouth. He wore a cap of the Tudor period and a vastly superior tunic, suggesting his importance over the other men.

Fennell also spoke of lost figures, including a man in possession of a great sword. He went on to refer to the representation of the hound and the stag, which Walker wrote of. And this, Fennell concluded, made the purpose of the house, and the vocation of its earliest inhabitants, quite clear. They were concerned with hunting, and the house was obviously the seat of the gentleman who was depicted in the tunic. This figure had his hand raised to his mouth because he was probably encouraging his dogs, in his role as chief huntsman.

In such times, suburban Wakefield did not exist; instead the house would have been located within what Fennell suggested was 'fine forest ground', with the Skitterick stream that flowed through the estate providing a ready source of refreshment for thirsty dogs as well as a home to families of otters. It seems these animals had lived in Wakefield for many centuries, for the parish's old churchwardens' accounts reveal that church officials were keen to remove the 'vermin' from the churchyard, and paid good money for their elimination.

Fennell concluded his talk by conjuring with words a vibrant picture of life in those days:

> Re-clothe the ground with verdure – square out the old parterres – re-plant the yews without – hang the mid-day dining hall with spears and hunting horns and trophies of the chase – and hear that merry party come in from hawking in the open country. Then open your eyes, and let's be off to luncheon.

Hewitt imagined, with no evidence, that the building, which was located at the bottom of Legh Street (by the roundabout adjacent to the present-day Wilko store), was even greater in its antiquity. Writing in his book on the town, he suggested that the Six Chimneys displayed the construction skills of 'our forefathers of a thousand years ago'. He described a visit he'd made to the building on 17 January 1860, when he observed 'some heavy stone-work, which extended from the ground floor to the roof, but above that height the continuation was brickwork to the tops of

The Six Chimneys.

some chimneys.' Hewitt also explained his understanding of the original chimneys that had given the building its name:

> Originally, the chimney or chimneys were intended to be the mainstay of the whole building; but its walls are still firm, and would, if allowed to remain without being wilfully pulled down, last irrespective of the intended support of the chimneys, many, very many long years to come. These chimneys contained six fireplaces, and consisted of six flues from them. They closely adjoined each other, and the fireplaces never had ranges in them.

Hewitt was keen to point out that to supply a house with so many fires, Wakefield clearly once stood within wooded surroundings. He could only but imagine the number of old timber buildings that must have once lined Wakefield's medieval streets, remarking that if 'some of the people of Wakefield of 500 years ago' were recalled to life, 'they would not be able to tell that Wakefield of the present, *from appearances*, was built upon the same ground that Wakefield of the 14th century stood upon.'

Though Hewitt went to his grave whilst the old building still stood proudly, the very many years he hoped it would remain so were not to be. On 21 August 1940, the *Yorkshire Evening Post*, under the headline 'A Bit Of Old Wakefield', ran a short article about the fate of the old relic:

Six Chimneys [is] the noted Elizabethan house in Central Wakefield, which is threatened with destruction, from an antiquarian standpoint, by a proposal to remove the top storey and the beautiful oak frontage. It is five years since the Corporation first negotiated for the purchase of the Six Chimneys with the object of preserving it as a historical monument, and possibly with a view to using it as a museum. The Corporation declined to buy the property for £4,500. It was stated at the time that another £3,000 would be required for renovation and the Corporation did not feel justified in asking the ratepayers to meet such a cost.

Mr W. Hammond, the owner, now states that before he proceeds with the proposed alterations he is prepared for a purchase to be fixed by arbitration. There is no indication of what the Corporation's reactions to such an offer would be, though there is a real desire apparent to preserve the building if it can be done without too great a burden being thrown on the ratepayers.

The question of money has always proved a stumbling block, and Wakefield really seeks a public-spirited benefactor who would save this fine old house for the city.

Two views of the dilapidated interior of the Six Chimneys. *By courtesy of YAHS.*

Six Chimneys was built as a hunting lodge in 1556, when a forest extended from Leeds to Castleford and Halifax. On the beams of the gables are several remarkable carvings.

For many years the salvation of the building had been mooted, but not acted upon. And in 1937, following a serious blaze at the site, it became clear that the fate of the Six Chimneys had been sealed. The fire, which occurred that December, broke out in a single storey part of the building at the back of the property, which was used as a store by Mr Bell, the brush manufacturer. The alarm was raised when a woman, passing by, spotted the flames, and quickly brought the situation to the attention of Wakefield Fire Brigade. Destruction was averted owing to the good work of the attending firemen who confined the blaze to Bell's stores, to the ruination of all his brushes.

Then, on 16 May 1941, the building finally gave way. William Hammond had attempted to make the repairs himself but he only made the building unstable. Apparently, vibrations caused by a passing lorry were the final straw, and centuries of Wakefield history came tumbling down.

'SIX CHIMNEYS – Collapse of Ancient Building' cried the following day's headline in the *Yorkshire Post*. The article went on:

Six Chimneys, the building in Kirkgate, Wakefield, which is reputed to have been built in 1556, suddenly collapsed last night. It is three storeys high, and the top two storeys on one side collapsed on the bottom storey.

The owner of Six Chimneys is Mr W. Hammond, who has used the ground floor as a cycle shop for a number of years.

A demolition squad was called out after the crash, and a good deal of debris was carried away before darkness.

On a number of occasions the Corporation have been urged to purchase the building in order that it might be preserved as an historical monument. At one time or another, the Wakefield Historical Society, the Yorkshire Archaeological Society and the Society for the Protection of Ancient Buildings have interested themselves in its preservation, but the question of money always proved an obstacle.

A month later, an associate of the Royal Institute of British Architects, called William Bell, wrote a somewhat sniffy letter to the same newspaper, alleging that twenty years earlier he had urged the city's councillors to purchase the building. He claimed that his suggestion met with 'good-humoured contempt' before the town clerk told him that there was no reason to preserve 'such a rickety old building', especially, Mr Bell reckoned, because the southern end of the site was required for widening the street. At this, Bell wondered whether 'those street-widening and road-straightening enthusiasts … now welcome the destruction of our ancient treasures by Hitler's young gangsters.' He concluded his missive by asking whether the only public spirit surviving in Wakefield was 'of that variety which is kept in bottles for use at mayoral banquets?'

Of course, the idea of using an old Wakefield building as a living museum was taken up by the council in 1971 when they turned Clarke Hall into such an attraction, though the money ran out, and in 2014 the building was sold on the open market, and is now lying in private hands.

The site of the original Six Chimneys, with inset showing the sign of the modern-day Weatherspoon's the Six Chimneys public house, situated at the top of Lower Kirkgate.

Close to the site of the old building stands Peterson Road, named after Andrew Peterson, who had once owned the Six Chimneys. During the 1920s, numbers twenty-five and twenty-seven were occupied by Joe and John William Hargrave. They were brothers and Wakefield natives who overcame injury and personal tragedy to become champions of commerce, and in Joe's case, hold public office and promote the well-being of Wakefield society. Appropriately, for reasons that will become clear, John's house at number twenty-seven was called *Anchorage*, with a plaque displaying this name hanging proudly over the front door. The brothers owned a high-class drapers', milliners' and costumiers' shop at 160, 162 and 164 Kirkgate, known as Hargrave Bros. Presently, the furniture outlet Scartop occupies this fine Georgian building, but as the image opposite reveals, the firm Hargrave Bros was established in 1890.

An earlier incarnation of the business was set up by Joe the year before. He'd been born in Scott's Buildings in Sandal on 17 March 1868 to master mariner Joseph Arnold Hargrave, and Sarah Hargrave, née Rothery. Joe and John had an older brother, Arnold Jabez Hargrave, who'd followed in their father's footsteps by becoming a sea captain in the Merchant Navy, mainly transporting cargoes of salt across Europe and North America.

The top of a Hargrave Bros' bill.

In 1890, John, who was the youngest of the three, having been born in Wakefield in 1870, joined his brother, Arnold Jabez, on a voyage from London aboard a sailing ship named *Arthur*. John, who yearned for a life at sea, took the role of mate, whilst Arnold was master. According to crew lists, John was still registered with the vessel the following year, though he soon became the victim of a dreadful accident when he fell from the crow's nest of his ship, suffering terrible injuries to one of his legs. It never fully healed and John was confined to a wheelchair for the rest of his life. At just twenty, his prospects of a career in the Merchant Navy had come to a sudden, crushing halt.

As for Joe, he'd recently completed an apprenticeship at a large store called Pygmalion on Boar Lane in Leeds. This was followed by a spell back in Wakefield working at Eggleston's draper's in Cross Square. But aged just twenty-one, Joe decided what he really wanted was to establish his own shop, and in 1889 he began a ladies' outfitters from his first premises at 118 Kirkgate, across the road from the Six Chimneys, and close to the British Oak Inn. Before long he welcomed his injured brother to the business as an equal partner, and together they began to build a company that would ultimately corner a slice of Wakefield's women's clothing market, in a city where they faced stiff competition.

To begin with, Joe and John lived above their first shop with their parents, and were enumerated at the address in the 1891 census, taken on Sunday, 5 April. Many years later, Joe's daughter Hilda,

Kirkgate from George Street. *By courtesy of YAHS.*

writing about her father in a letter, described the shop's location. She said: 'Passing George Street it was the second shop on the left-hand side going up [Kirkgate], Agar's grocer's shop being next to it on the corner.' Hilda recalled that years later, Webster's music shop operated from Hargrave Bros' former site.

On 17 March 1892, Joe, by then a 24-year-old draper, of Kirkgate House, 118 Kirkgate, married Annie Wilson, daughter of carver and gilder George Wilson, of 11 Kirkgate. Their marriage took place at Salem Chapel on George Street, and was celebrated by Robert Stratten Holmes, the minister. It was in this year when the brothers acquired 176 Kirkgate, which stood near the Wellington Inn, but is now demolished. From here they ran a baby linen shop, Annie Hargrave taking a leading role in building up this part of the business.

Annie and Joe's first four children, Wilson, Edina, Irene and Raymond Hargrave, were born above this shop in 1893, 1894, 1896 and 1899, respectively. Tragically, Wilson only lived for two days, and Edina succumbed to a bout of pneumonia on 18 August 1895, aged just eighteenth months. Later that decade, on 8 November 1899, the brothers lost their father, Joseph Arnold Hargrave. He'd died while convalescing in Blackpool, where Arnold Jabez and his wife Caroline were running a hotel from 20 Station Road. He'd lived long enough to meet his grandson, Raymond, who'd been born on 17 April that year. But while at his Uncle John's home at *Anchorage* on Peterson Road, the little boy fell victim to adenitis and died on 10 April 1902, just a week before his third birthday. Irene wasn't to remain an only child, for her sister, Hilda, was born on 19 August 1904 at Joe's new house, 25 Peterson Road, also known as *Lyndholme*, a semi-detached property adjoining John's *Anchorage*.

On 19 September 1906, at Oxford Place Methodist Chapel, John, aged thirty-six, married 27-year-old Sarah Elizabeth Walker, and the couple began a family of their own, with three daughters, Nora, Evelyn and Lilian (who died in infancy), and a son, Eric, all born in Wakefield.

In about 1910, the brothers opened their largest shop at 160–164 Kirkgate, occupying half of the building. They initially retained the 176 Kirkgate site before eventually moving in to the whole of the premises at 160–164, the only one of the three Hargrave Bros' sites where the building still stands.

In April 1928, the publication *Dress & Coiffure: A review of fashion's progress* ran an article about the business in which Kirkgate was described as 'the busy main street of that prosperous

118 Kirkgate. *By courtesy of David Smith.*   176 Kirkgate. *By courtesy of David Smith.*

Yorkshire city, Wakefield'. The business was said to have increased 'its already great hold on the shopping public of the town and district, and, in general is exhibiting all those signs which indicate that a business holds the complete confidence of its clientele.' The article also focused on Joe's contribution to public life. He was a justice of the peace from 1917 onwards; president of the Wakefield District Chamber of Trade in 1916 and 1917, having been a member since 1894, and was also president of the Wakefield Tradesmen's Benevolent Institution in 1935, when he increased subscriptions by £50. He was a director of the Wakefield Mutual Plate Glass Company, and president of the Wakefield Naturalists' Society. He'd also served as a Wakefield councillor (as a Liberal), with a brief stint on the sanitary committee, and had encouraged his plumber nephew, Arnold Hargrave (Arnold Jabez's son), to follow in his political footsteps. In 1927, Arnold junior, standing in the Kirkgate Ward as a Socialist, duly beat Conservative George Hemingway, the owner of an omnibus company, into second place.

   As for Joe's personal interests, these were varied. He was involved with the Wakefield Historical Society, the Paxton Society, and was the honorary librarian at the Wakefield Institute of Literature and Science based at the old Mechanics' Institute on Wood Street. He worshipped at the old

Zion Chapel shown in the late nineteenth century. *By courtesy of YAHS.*

Zion Chapel in 2015. The building now comprises private apartments.

Zion Congregational Church on nearby George Street (now converted into flats), where he was treasurer and secretary for many years.

As for his business, it was said locally that 'if you wanted to be seen, you were seen in Hargrave Bros', and indeed, the 1928 article described the stock as 'first-class at fair prices, offering the best value for the quality on offer'. The shop boasted several sections including a mantle department, which was said to be equal to the millinery department; there was also a glove department, but the main offering was the dresses. These were made in Yorkshire in some of the many textile mills the county once boasted. Ladies' and children's outfitting departments were accompanied by a baby linen section, and soft furnishings were also available such as curtains, tablecloths, towels etc.

But despite the continued growth of the business, it would not last another four years, for on 23 January 1932, John, who had grown weaker as the years had taken their toll on his frail body, died, aged just sixty-one. He left a widow, two grown-up daughters, and an 18-year-old son.

Joe did not continue in business, soon selling all the firm's stock to Rowell's, a clothing company based in Derbyshire, which would eventually take over from Hargrave Bros at the Kirkgate site. One of their adverts read: 'If saving money means anything to you don't miss … Rowell's GREAT

STOCK SALE.' The sale, held at their Chesterfield shop, commenced on 1 July 1932, just six months after John's death. The advert for the sale, which appeared in several northern newspapers, including the *Derbyshire Times*, announced that the company had just 'purchased the stock of Messrs Hargrave Bros General Drapers, Kirkgate, Wakefield' and that Rowell's would 'clear the whole of it at Knock-out Prices. Wonderful Bargains in all Departments.'

Joe remained active in public life right up to his death. He was one of the guarantors for the Pageant of Wakefield and the West Riding, which was held in the city in 1933, and his obituary titled 'Death of a Wakefield Magistrate, Mr Joe Hargrave. A Long and Honourable Life' was published in the *Wakefield Express* in January 1941. It included tributes from several of Wakefield's leading lights. Mr J.A. Yonge spoke for the city magistrates and said that Joe would 'rank among the worthiest of Wakefield citizens', that he'd led an honourable life, loved the city, and 'never spared himself in its service', adding that he felt privileged to have been closely associated with him for a number of years. Local solicitor Mr Thomas Edward Catterall said Joe had been a 'conscientious magistrate' and that he echoed Mr Yonge's sentiments. The chief constable in those days was

160–164 Kirkgate shown in May 1926, when it won best window in Wakefield during British Empire Shopping week. *By courtesy of David Smith.*

Scarptop, a furniture store housed within the former Hargrave Bros shop.

Mr Robert Yelloly. He said that he had known Joe ever since he (Yelloly) came to Wakefield, 'and our associations were always of the best, and I will miss him very much, as we all will.'

Joe's funeral was held at the Zion Chapel, attended by the mayor, the town clerk, and many other Wakefield officials. It was conducted by Reverend Courtney, who spoke about the Bible Reading Classes that Joe had held as a young man at the old Salem Chapel, formerly on George Street, where he'd married. Finally, he told the congregation that Joe was not only interested in seeing justice properly administered, but also with the concept of the rehabilitation of offenders, which he helped to promote through his membership of the Discharged Prisoners' Aid Society and the Wakefield City Mission.

The Hargraves moved home frequently when Joe and John were children, while their father was away for long periods on his merchant ships. After leaving Sandal, the family had settled on Thornhill Street in the Kirkgate area of Wakefield, close to Hargrave Square, where they rented small properties to local families. The square was situated close to New Wells, where it is said that the medicinal spring waters once found there almost led to Wakefield becoming a rival to the great spa towns of the country. But such a feat was not to be achieved.

Joe and John William Hargrave taking tea with their sister, Anne Elizabeth Hancock, and John's daughter, Evelyn. *By courtesy of David Smith.*

An article appeared in the *Yorkshire Evening Post* on 14 August 1924 claiming to cite the views of a former native of the city who had long since packed his bags and decamped to America. The critic, as he was termed in the report, had reckoned that Wakefield had lost its chance to become 'the industrial and social capital of the West Riding as well as nominally being the administrative centre'. The piece attempted to draw attention to the city's lost potential, the journalist citing an unsourced quote from an 'official document' that he claimed was 200 years old, and had stated that the Wakefield of olden times was 'nowe … the greatest markett and prinicpall place of resorte of all sorts of Clothiers Drapers and other Traffikers for Cloath in all theis parts'. In actual fact the citation came from a letter written by four West Riding justices of the peace sitting at the General Sessions held in Wakefield in 1628. But why then, asked the ill-informed journalist, had Wakefield, so revered in olden times, shown such a lack of foresight ever since? One such 'lost chance' concerned Wakefield's one-time fame as an unofficial spa town. 'One hundred and fifty years ago,' the journalist told his readers, 'it was famous as a spa, and with proper management might have proved a serious rival to Harrogate.' He went on:

Wakefield's one-time popularity as a spa has still a memorial in New Wells, now the centre of a furnishing business. The New Wells were situated at the bottom of Thornhill Street, and mineral waters from those wells were especially good for weak eyes and deranged stomachs.

A hydropathic institution sprang up on the site, and it only needed a Dr Jeffrey, who established the fame of Leamington, or a Lord North, who discovered Tunbridge Wells, to puff the virtues of the chalybeate, but no such individual arose, and after a brief flicker of popularity the fame of Wakefield's wells died out, leaving but the name to bear testimony to yet another chance that had been lost.

The bare facts are true: there was indeed such a spa at the lower end of Thornhill Street, and this was written about by Crowther in 1886. In fact, the journalist may well have been thinking of his own copy of Crowther's short book when he purloined some of Crowther's phrases and used them in his own article: 'puff the virtues of the chalybeate' and the references to Jeffrey and North, being lifted straight from the original text, almost word for word.

Reverend Thomas Kilby, the nineteenth-century incumbent of St John's Church, described himself as an amateur artist, and in 1843 he produced a collection of drawings that he published as *Scenery in the Vicinity of Wakefield*. One of his lithographs was described as 'Trinity Church and New Wells'.

Kilby also included notes with his drawings, and of New Wells he wrote:

Trinity Church and New Wells, by Reverend Kilby.

The New Wells site today, shown from Charlotte Street.

The old building a little to the left of the church was formerly a bath; and there are persons still living in the town who remember it to have been held in great estimation by the inhabitants on account of its strengthening qualities. A few years since, the following Latin inscription was visible over the entrance-door: '*Fontes, benedicte Deo*'; it is now entirely concealed by the ivy which hangs in graceful masses over that part of the house.

Crowther explained that 'the Wells were in the part of the house now used as a kitchen, and there was a spring also outside the house as now.' The area is at least remembered in name by New Wells Terrace and the retirement homes that bear the name New Wells, though medicinal spas gave way to industry and commerce, and a furnishing shop was opened on the site before housing eventually replaced the once popular attraction.

There was another medicinal spa to be found on the outskirts of the town, behind Clarke Hall, on the way to Stanley. It was named St Swithin's Well and stood beside the Chantry Chapel of St Swithun that was once located in this area at a place known as Wodewell. An article that featured in the *Wakefield Express* in 1949 described 'a small cottage which stands in the fields at the rear of Clarke Hall, Stanley', the only surviving relic of a 'noted medicinal spa'. The newspaper went on to confirm that the spa had dried up ninety-seven years previously. The well was named in the 1832 Parliamentary Act when the new constituency boundaries of Wakefield were defined as a result of the Reform Act, and Hilary Marland discusses the well in her book, *Medicine and Society in Wakefield and Huddersfield 1780–1870*. The *Express* article stated that 'at the height of its fame St Swithin's Well was known throughout the district and people came from far and near to bathe in its ice-cold water which was said to have had a curative effect, particularly in tubercular diseases.' With a keen eye for a business opportunity, Sir Michael Pilkington, of Stanley Hall, built a bath house at the location, employed a permanent caretaker and housed him in a cottage. Paying customers enjoyed a large-sized bath, of around 10 feet square, complete with benches around the sides, from where they could sit and dip their toes before stepping into the soothing water, which reached their shoulders. With a description that sounds more like a modern spa than an eighteenth-century visitor attraction, the paper told its readers that:

> Entrance to the bath was through a large archway in the caretaker's cottage and down a flight of steps into the basement. There was also a dressing room for the use of the visitors. A frequent bather at St Swithin's Well was Rev Samuel Sharp, Vicar of Wakefield.

Wakefield has not been short of its fair share of rainwater, and over the years the town has been subjected to some notable floods, not least in 1866, when it was hit by so much rain that over 2 feet of standing water remained after the downpour had ceased, surpassing a record set in 1837. The areas around Kirkgate, notably by the banks of the Calder, came in for quite a battering.

The rain that had been beating down began worsening on Thursday, 15 November 1866, increasing in volume overnight, until that Friday saw an immense downpour that was falling on many towns and cities across Lancashire and Yorkshire. Wakefield was hit severely. On 17 November 1866, London newspaper *The Morning Post* told its readers of 'great floods in the north'. Manchester had also been badly affected, the river Irwell 'swollen to a fearful height' and at Salford, parts of the low ground 'for 500 or 600 acres' were completely under water. At Wakefield, the paper told how the banks of the river Calder had become a 'scene of intense excitement'.

> The heavy rains of Thursday and the previous days had caused the river to rise to an almost unprecedented height, and flood the surrounding neighbourhood. Two vessels were carried over the damstakes and two men drowned. Shortly afterwards a jetty in the front of a warehouse gave way, and a sloop moored to it was let loose and went swiftly down the stream. It struck first against a vessel on the left bank, giving a sudden twist round, and then flew with great velocity over the damstakes and struck against the bridge below shaking the buttresses to their foundations. The other vessel had previously gone over. The banks of the river were lined with people. The river rose until the water above and below the dam was on a level, and until there was but a small portion of the arches of the bridge visible; and the captains were taking advantage of this to float

their emptied vessels back over the wear. At a late hour in the afternoon they had not succeeded. The Manchester corn factors never reached the market at all, in consequence of a line on the tunnel being flooded.

As the days progressed, the stories became gloomier and more disturbing. The *Wakefield Express* reminded readers of the floods of December 1837, which had hit Kirkgate, but this present turmoil, the paper confirmed, had seen an even greater body of water lash that part of the town. A Lancashire publication, *The Ashton Weekly Reporter*, described in more detail the loss of the two lives referred to in *The Morning Post*. The disaster happened on Thornes Lane when William Armstrong, captain of a Beverley keel called *Peace*, which was laden with wheat, began moving his boat to the flour mill run by Mr J. Fawcett.

TWO MEN DROWNED – Between eight and nine o'clock on Friday morning a sad calamity occurred on the Calder, which, even at that early hour, had risen to an almost unprecedented height. The captain of a keel named the *Peace*, of Beverley, was lowering his vessel down to Mr J. Fawcett's flour mill, for the purpose of delivering a cargo of wheat, when the rope broke, and the boat drifted on to the damstakes. A small boat was then sent out to the vessel with some more ropes, when it was upset and two men, named Amos Bates, and William Hepworth, the former a miller at Mr Fawcett's, and the latter a corn porter, were thrown into the water, and Bates was carried away by the stream, while Hepworth contrived to reach the shore. As the mate of the vessel was endeavouring to pass along two ropes from the vessel to the shore, he was also carried away by the force of the water, and both men were drowned. The boat went over the damstakes, and about noon it was followed by another which ran into a vessel, and also against the Kirkgate Bridge with great force. After they had been unloaded, they were got over the damstakes with some difficulty. Several other vessels, it was stated, had been stranded higher up the river, the telegraph wires were broken down, and the lower parts of the town and the neighbourhood of the Ings Beck were completely inundated. The tremendous nature of the flood caused great crowds to assemble on the banks of the river and upon the bridge.

The Wakefield paper described the areas of the town that had been hit the worst, with Thornes Lane, Ings Road, the bottom end of Westgate, and Denby Dale cited. Houses on Ings Road and Grove Street (adjacent to Grove Road) were completely flooded, with 5 feet of water visible through the windows, and those not at home when the heaviest rain fell had no hope of salvaging their possessions. Transport was hastily arranged to convey people to their homes, and even for those who just wanted to take a tour of the flooded town.

By 19 November, the *Yorkshire Post and Leeds Intelligencer* reported that the water, which had reached 2 feet and half an inch, was finally beginning to subside. The height achieved was a record for the time and was 'obtained with such exactitude' because the previous record high, following rainfall on 21 December 1837, had been 'marked upon the walls of the Old Soke Mills, abutting upon the stream.'

The Leeds paper declared that the 'spectacle at the Kirkgate end of the town is an awful one,' with miles of land devastated, and an estimation of a huge bill of about £50,000 just to repair the damage done to the town alone, not to mention the areas surrounding it, such as Horbury and Stanley. The *London Evening Standard*, in its 21 November edition, reckoned it would cost double that figure to remedy the damage done to Wakefield. And that was half of the £200,000 thought to be the sum required to reverse the carnage wrought on the entire Calder vale district.

The flood of December 1837, remembered by the *Wakefield Express* and the *Yorkshire Post* during their coverage of the chaos of 1866, also hit the headlines, and this evoked John Hewitt's memories. He described the chaos of 1837 as 'St Thomas' Flood', recalling how he'd been in Leeds at the time, witnessing first-hand the damage the rain had caused there. By 23 December, news of the calamity had reached the offices of the *York Herald* newspaper. Word travelled rather slower in those days, the first railway station not opening in York until 1839, and the reporter could only guess that the heavy rain had caused an 'enormous extent' of damage. The reporter had learned that on Brooksbank on Westgate (where an elderly lady would carry her bed-ridden husband to safety on her back during the floods of 1866) inhabitants had been forced to quit the lower levels of their homes, after just an hour's rain. Instead, they had to 'take refuge in the upper stories, the water reaching, in some instances, to the fire-places, and quenching the fire.'

But from what he had gleaned, the York-based reporter stated that Kirkgate had come off worst of all. Water had filled the cellars of three pubs, causing barrels to bob about, doing no good whatsoever to the contents as they crashed into each other, cracking the oaken casks and spilling the publicans' livelihoods to create a gloomy sea of ale-tinged rainwater and floating wood. Pigs, sheep and cattle were lost, and a horse was found 'lodged against Kirkgate-bridge, with several immense piles of wood, supposed to have formed parts of wooden bridges, or supports of weirs, or dams, belonging to the tributary streams to the Calder.' A keel carrying a cargo of corn became detached from its mooring at Kirkgate and was propelled by the water, cargo and all, over the bridge. It was also reported, in the *Leeds Intelligencer*, that the Corn Market, held at Wakefield the day after the flood, had been stopped 'by the greatest flood experienced for several years' and that it was anticipated that normal business would not resume for several days.

As the facts began to fall into place, a clearer picture emerged of the devastation wreaked by the flood. On Christmas morning the *London Standard* ran a story it had obtained from the *West Riding Herald*, which declared that the inhabitants of Wakefield had 'witnessed one of the most sudden and disastrous floods ever remembered.' Rain hit in the afternoon over Horbury and though 'several persons in Thornes-lane and Kirkgate' had warning of the oncoming downpour, it was stated that they did nothing to prepare for the onslaught, not expecting conditions to turn so nasty, so quickly. But later that evening, about eight o'clock, water came crashing out of Thornes Lane, reaching the cellar of the Spotted Dog Inn at the bottom of Kirkgate, opposite the Grey Horse, by ten o'clock, and entering warehouses and private dwellings along the way. Surely this would be the extent of the tide? No such luck. It wasn't until six in the morning that the water finally began to subside, by which time it had already reached the Ship Inn.

The 'Old Ship Hotel', Kirkgate (otherwise Old Ship Inn), which stood on a site by the modern-day junction with Ings Road (close to the junction with Grove Road), where Ship Yard still survives. In this image the name of the publican, Charles Hubert Salmon, a Horbury-born man who held the licence in the early 1900s, can be seen above the doorway on the right. Mr Salmon later ran the Bull Hotel on Westgate. In November 1915 it was reported in the *Yorkshire Evening Post* that one Henry Hubert Heath, a wagon builder 'of no fixed abode', had been charged with breaking and entering the Old Ship Inn. A servant girl had found Heath asleep in a cellar 'in a drunken condition … around him were seven empty pint beer bottles and other full bottles were in his pockets.' The paper concluded that Heath had gained access via the trap door and shoot.

The next day, before about one o'clock in the afternoon, the streets were beginning to clear of water and anguished voices were gradually replaced by the sound of boisterous laughter as good spirits returned. But soon there was further trouble, for a vessel by the name of *Liberty*, which had been heading for the warehouse run by the Fernandes brothers, was found to have been carried over the dam stones and suffered a leak, at the loss of all the wheat it was carrying. The townsfolk rushed to help, clearing the mess in less than four hours, during which labours somebody spotted a barrel of porter floating by. This was immediately seized, tapped and enjoyed by the thirsty salvagers. They attempted to get the vessel back above the dam stones, but this would have to wait, for not a single arch of the bridge could be discerned, the entirety being submerged.

Back on Thornes Lane, Mr Mellin, a local dyer, reported losses of no less than £700, and damage to the corn warehouses of Dunn, Fernandes, Kelshaw, Alder, Hansell, Gosney and others, by the banks of the river, was estimated to be about £4,000. Flagstones and paving stones were lifted, and the sewers were opened up as 'every possible means' was taken 'to facilitate the retreat of the water.' As the clean-up operation swung into action further loss was uncovered.

James Craven's boatyard had opened in 1825. Part of the business was carried out on the site of the present Hepworth Gallery, whilst a saw pit and stove were situated just below the basin of the Calder and Hebble Navigation. Materials from Craven's boatyard had 'got afloat', though when the newspaper was printed the cost of the damage wasn't known. He certainly recovered from the damage, continuing successfully in the boat-building trade until he sold his business in 1856. Mercifully, unlike in 1866, no lives were lost in the great flood of 1837.

The water on the river froze in January 1855, during a cold snap that lasted for six weeks. Newspapers reported that the Aire and Calder and Calder and Hebble navigations were closed because of it, thus effecting deliveries to the Corn Market, though by now the railways offered alternative means for transporting stock to and from the market. Hewitt reckoned that games of football and cricket were played on the frozen river at this time, as people were unable to work, and so found ways to amuse themselves. One man thought he'd quite like to board one of the boats, which was moored at Thornes Lane Wharf. So off he went across the ice, right up to it, 'not thinking that the ice had been broken in alongside the vessel.' Of course, as he reached the

Thornes Lane Wharfe today.

Castle Bank Mills, a little further upriver, by Henry Clarke. *By courtesy WLSL.*

vessel, he found he no longer had a firm footing, and promptly disappeared from view, before resurfacing and plunging below again in an instant. Hewitt, who witnessed the incident, reported that a waterman fished him out with a boat hook before helping him back on to land. Drenched, and a little ashamed, he was subjected to ridicule from assembled bystanders, before turning on his heels and tramping home, quite soaked.

The site of the bridge of nine arches over the river Calder, upon which stands the ancient Chantry Chapel, can boast its fair share of extraordinary tales. It's thought that a flood had destroyed an earlier wooden bridge in the 1340s, and between 1342 and 1356, a new stone bridge, with the chapel, was built in its place. The bridge has been widened to about three times its original width of 10 feet and the chapel frontage restored in the nineteenth and twentieth centuries, the latter restoration necessary because architect George Gilbert Scott had used Caen stone to carve the new façade in the 1840s. This material did not hold up well to the soot and grime polluting the air during the Victorian age.

A very early view of the bridge and chapel was painted by Wakefield artist George Fleming and engraved in 1743 by William Henry Toms. The painting is called *A PERSPECTIVE VIEW of the CHAPELL adjoining to WAKEFIELD BRIDGE in the COUNTY of YORK*, and of the original prints, very few survive, though a copy of one is shown below, and provides a glimpse of how the scene appeared before the restoration of a century later.

The Yorkshire Architectural Society oversaw the restoration work after the chapel had been returned to the Church of England in 1842, some 500 years after the original building work was believed to have begun. It was this earlier year, 1342, when Edward III had allowed the bailiffs of Wakefield to charge a toll on all passing trade and animals crossing the bridge. This toll was granted in order to help the townsfolk pay for repairs to their broken bridge.

The chapel would have been a welcome sight to travellers coming in to the town, and until the Abolition of Chantries, following Acts of Parliament passed in 1545 and 1547, masses would have been sung for the dead by chantry priests. After this, the building was put to secular use, and for almost 300 years it served several functions. According to the *York Herald* of 25 July 1891, 'it has been degraded into an old clothes shop, a warehouse, a shop for flax dressers, a newsroom, a cheesecake house, and a tailor's shop.' It was also used as the office of a corn factor; it was held for a time by George Fleming, the abovementioned painter, and used by him as a dwelling; and was even used to store water.

Adverts began to appear in 1842 inviting architects to tender their bids for the restoration work, and on 19 November 1842 the *Leeds Intelligencer* included the following notice in their publication:

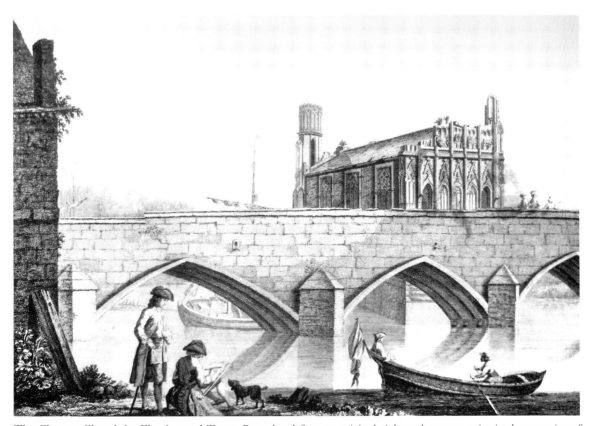

The Chantry Chapel, by Fleming and Toms. *Reproduced from an original eighteenth-century print in the possession of Wakefield company, Heir Line Ltd.*

YORKSHIRE ARCHITECTURAL SOCIETY

THE RESTORATION of the ANCIENT CHANTRY on WAKEFIELD BRIDGE having been committed to the Yorkshire Architectural Society, by the Rev Samuel Sharp, Vicar of Wakefield;

ARCHITECTS are requested to SEND IN, ON OR BEFORE FEB 1st NEXT, ESTIMATES, SPECIFICATIONS, PLANS, ELEVATIONS, & SECTIONS, with Details, a quarter the Size of the Original, to SAML WILKINSON, Hon Sec

15, Wellington-Street, Leeds.

The Enclosures must be Signed with a Motto, and accompanied by a Sealed Note bearing the same Motto, containing the Architect's name.

Gilbert Scott won the contest and the chapel was opened for religious services in 1848.

The bridge features in an enduring legend concerning the Battle of Wakefield (part of the so-called Wars of the Roses), which took place near to Sandal Castle on 30 December 1460. The opponents were the Yorkists on one side, led by Richard, Duke of York, and on the other were the Lancastrian forces, of Margaret of Anjou, wife of the reigning monarch, Henry VI. King Henry was prone to bouts of serious mental breakdown, perhaps schizophrenia, and in

South-east view of the chapel and bridge, by Reverend Kilby.

Another view of the chapel, by Reverend Kilby.

King Edward the Third's Chapel, by Sam Topham.

August 1453 he had a severe mental collapse, which temporarily robbed him of his power of speech and left him existing in an almost trance-like state. As the king was now incapacitated, the following March, Richard was named as Lord Protector of the realm, much to the fury of Henry's wife. The king recovered by Christmas 1454 and Richard was relieved of his role. But in May the following year, Richard captured Henry at the relatively minor Battle of St Albans and was soon restored to the office of protector, amid rumours that Henry was ill again. The second protectorate did not last long, coming to an end in February 1456, with Margaret now apparently in control of her husband. Then, in 1460, following the climax of the Battle of Northampton, at which the Yorkists had claimed a decisive victory, Henry, who had again been taken prisoner, was forced to give way to Richard once more, and the Duke of York was appointed Lord Protector for a third time. As a result, the king was forced to agree to the Act of Accord. This meant that he could continue to reign, but his second cousin, Richard, Duke of York, was to succeed him, in spite of Henry having a legitimate heir: his son, Prince Edward. Parliament passed the Act on 25 October 1460, conceding that Richard's genealogical claim to the throne was better than Henry's. Queen Margaret was never going to take this lightly, and was outraged that her son, Edward, would not succeed his father. So, she gathered her forces and they marched to Sandal, near Wakefield, where Richard was spending Christmas 1460. Richard was hopelessly outnumbered: some historians suggest there were several thousand Lancastrians to just a few hundred Yorkists. For reasons never made clear, Richard left the stronghold of his castle to face the might of the Lancastrian army on the battlefield, where his forces were routed and he was slain.

In scene four of the first act of *King Henry VI Part 3*, Shakespeare has Queen Margaret openly taunting Richard before he is stabbed to death by John, Lord Clifford. Then the Queen places a paper crown on Richard's head and at the end of the act orders his decapitation with the lines: 'Off with his head, and set it on York gates; So York may overlook the town of York.'

This is not quite true; whilst it is believed that Richard's head, wearing a paper crown, was placed atop Micklegate Bar in York, apparently complete with a sign reading 'Let York overlook the town of York', the Queen was not at Wakefield at the time of the battle, nor even in Yorkshire, being in Scotland during December 1460. But less contested is the legend of the death of Richard's 17-year-old son, Edmund, Earl of Rutland, who fled the battle alongside his tutor, Robert Aspell, with Clifford in hot pursuit. Clifford apparently caught up with Rutland as he crossed the bridge, passing the chantry, and ignoring his pleas for mercy, stabbed the young price to death in revenge for the death of his own father, at the hands of Richard, Duke of York.

Thomas Baines, writing in his 1871 publication *Yorkshire Past and Present*, gave an edited account of what Leland said on the matter, following the antiquary's visit in 1538:

> There was a sore battle fought in the South Fields by this bridge; and in the flight of the duke of
> York's party, either the duke himself, or his son the earl of Rutland, was slain a little above the

bars beyond the bridge going up to the town of Wakefield, that standeth full fairly upon a diving (sloping or rather ascending) ground. At this place is set up a cross in memory of the event, in *rei memoriam*. The common saying is there that the earl would have (wished to have) taken (refuge) in a poor woman's house for succour, and that she for fear shut the door, and straight the earl was killed. The Lord Clifford, for killing of men at this battle, was called the butcher.

Following their burials at Pontefract, the bodies of Richard and Edmund were removed to Fotheringhay Castle in Northamptonshire in July 1476. In July 2010, in the year of the 550th anniversary of the Battle of Wakefield, Wakefield Historical Society arranged a special journey to Fotheringhay, following the route Richard's body took when it was conveyed, with Edmund's, from Pontefract for reburial. Events were scheduled to run from 21 July to 29 July 2010, the latter being the recorded date of the reburial itself. The programme began at Sandal Castle, now a sad ruin, where Richard Knowles, Fellow of the Society of Antiquaries, gave a talk entitled *The Battle of Wakefield and the Duke of York Monument*. The monument, which includes a depiction the Duke of York, was erected in 1897 on the supposed site where he fell. It is thought that it replaced an earlier memorial, which was probably removed by Oliver Cromwell's troops. It can be found on Manygates Lane, in front of an adult education centre, which was formerly a school. The monument was funded by public subscription, and the project was overseen by J.W. Walker. In recent years it was vandalized, the perpetrator removing the Duke of York's head. Perhaps the vandal was a descendent of Lord Clifford and still bore this ancient grudge. Happily, the duke has been restored, and the words carved below can still be read clearly:

> Richard Plantagenet Duke of York fighting for the cause of the White Rose fell on this spot in the Battle of Wakefield December 30: 1460. This stone is erected in 1897 by some who wish to preserve the traditional site.

The events of 21 July 2010 then continued at the Chantry Chapel, where the late Wakefield historian, Kate Taylor MBE, gave a talk. Following this, Dr Phil

Richard, Duke of York Monument. *By courtesy of YAHS.*

Chantry Chapel from the Hepworth.

Judkins spoke at St Giles' Church, Pontefract, and the following day, after a tour of Pontefract Castle, it was on to Doncaster, and eventually, on 29 July, to Fotheringhay Castle.

Henry Clarkson, in the second edition of his book *Memories of Merry Wakefield*, talked about Titus Salt and the famous manufacturer's connection to Wakefield. He suggested that Sir Titus had initially considered, as a location for his huge mill, a site on the banks of the river Calder, at the bottom of Kirkgate, near where Mr Mellin ran his dye works. But, of course, he chose the site near Shipley where he built his model village of Saltaire, opening the mill there in 1853. Reverend Robert Balgarnie wrote *Sir Titus Salt, Baronet, His life and its lessons*, which he published in 1877, shortly after Salt's death. In the book he wrote that it was doubtful that Wakefield was ever an option for Sir Titus, inferring that the 'peaceful and beautiful' surroundings that he eventually chose were more suited to his plans than the once pumping, industrial heart of the woollen trade.

But Salt's early Wakefield connections are interesting all the same. He attended a school at Salem Chapel Yard on George Street and was a classmate of Henry Clarkson. Titus had been born in 1803 in Morley, where he was baptised at the Independent New Old Chapel, prior to a second baptism at the Anglican St Peter's Church, Batley. His father, Daniel Salt, was a drysalter, who removed the family to Crofton where they kept a farm. Their former Crofton home is now the Goose and Cowslip public house.

George Street during a Cattle Market, by Henry Clarke. *By courtesy WLSL.*

Clarkson told his readers:

Amongst my schoolfellows was one whose name has since become very famous; I allude to the late Sir Titus Salt. His father, Mr Daniel Salt, occupied a small farm at Crofton, and his son rode the 4 miles to school every day on a donkey, bringing his dinner with him in a basket. He was not one of the most genial companions, and seldom would join in our sports and games at the noon-day hour, preferring to spend the time apart, in solitary thought, a characteristic which I understand clung to him through life, and no doubt had much to do with his steady tide of prosperity.

Despite there being some apparent doubt among biographers about the schools that Titus Salt attended, it appears quite clear that in his young life he was a pupil at the school at the end of Salem Chapel Yard. Clarkson described one of the masters there as an Independent Minister named Reverend Benjamin Rayson. Rayson was a widower, who one day, in 1815, turned up to class dressed in his finest apparels, 'silk stockings, smart shoes and buckles, and a new suit of black clothes'. Rayson promptly gave the children the day off, telling them Reverend Sharp (of pigeon fame) had just married him to Mrs Fenton, a rich widow. This marriage was actually celebrated on

The Goose and Cowslip public house, Crofton, formerly the Salts' home.

26 March 1816, and the teacher soon left the employment of the school, to live, as Clarkson put it, 'in clover'.

Reverend Balgarnie explained that the nearest place of worship that suited the Salt family's religious preferences was the Independents' Congregational Salem Chapel, some 3 miles from Crofton, on George Street in Kirkgate. Reverend Rayson was the minister, and it was through this connection that the young Titus began attending the associated school. Balgarnie said:

> But his secular education had yet to be acquired. He had now arrived at the age of eleven, and was sent by his father to the day school connected with Salem Chapel, Wakefield; the Rev B. Rayson, along with the duties of his pastorate, uniting those of a schoolmaster. The school was held in a building adjoining the chapel in George-street, now used as a printing-office.

Reverend Balgarnie cited a letter written by a school friend of Sir Titus. The correspondent may have been Henry Clarkson for some of the details in the letter are similar to the account given in Clarkson's book. The donkey he rode on (which was tethered at the nearby Nags Head Inn while he studied), the dinner contained in a basket, and Titus's prevailing state of quietude, were all mentioned.

In his own book, Clarkson stated that Reverend Rayson was succeeded at the school by Enoch Harrison, of whom Clarkson said, he 'always had a great respect, notwithstanding one or two sound thrashings which he administered to me.'

In 1820, when his school days were over, Titus went to work at Joseph Jackson's four-storey wool stapling warehouse on King Street.

Two years later, following the expiration of the lease on his family's farm, Titus moved with his father to Bradford, working at Rouse and Son Mill before he went into business with the elder man, styling their firm Daniel Salt & Son, and as Reverend Balgarnie put it, 'thus his connection with Wakefield was brought to a close, and Bradford was henceforth to become the scene of his remarkable course in life.'

In 1833, Titus succeeded his father in the family business, and soon began experimenting with alpaca wool, making from this shimmering material fine outfits to be worn by the wives of wealthy husbands. This venture proved immensely successful, and in 1850 he decided to erect a custom-built mill. But where would he choose to build it?

A legend persists that Wakefield was his first choice. According to the legend, which was discussed by J.W. Walker, among others, Titus Salt returned to the town to look at a site close to the dye works once occupied by Mr Mellin, but his plans were scuppered owing to factors that had caused the decline of Wakefield's woollen industry during the nineteenth century. In his history of Wakefield, Walker wrote about the decline, citing commentary made by Reverend Camidge. He had said that at the beginning of the century, the aristocracy of Wakefield, these being its merchant princes, refused to permit the building of new mills in the town, yet they were 'well content to ride in their carriages and four, and attend the markets in other towns, but would not have manufacture brought to Wakefield.' He insisted that this led to manufacturers setting up in Leeds, and further restrictions forbade those who had apprenticed in Wakefield from setting up new businesses within first 7, then 10 miles of the town, which led to the emergence of Bradford as an important woollen centre. Walker stated that the merchant princes, the Heywood, Milnes and Naylor families, did not want their connection with the Russian textile market to be severed by any rivals, hence their reluctance to aid, in any way, new business. And Walker also suggested that opposition in the 1850s chased away Titus Salt.

It is said that when Sir Titus Salt (then Mr Salt) was looking out for a site for his mill to manufacturer alpaca, he decided upon settling it in the Ings, but so much opposition was raised to the scheme by some of the inhabitants that he betook himself to Bradford and there founded the great industrial centre of Saltaire.

Of course, Sir Titus was already established in Bradford, and it seems that it was more likely that limited space would have scuppered any chance of him setting up a village named Saltcalder on the banks of the river in Wakefield. Clarkson alluded to this in his book:

Greenwood House, where Salem Chapel Yard once stood, showing Morrison's supermarket, part of the Ridings shopping centre.

I have heard it stated, that before building his extensive works at Saltaire, he came to Wakefield in search of a suitable site, and looked at some premises near the river, formerly used by Mr Mellin, as Dye Works; but Mr Salt abandoned the idea of building there, as the area of land was not large enough for his requirements. The works in question were afterwards purchased by Messrs Hodgson and Simpson, and form part of their extensive premises. The acquaintance between Sir Titus Salt and myself was continued through life whenever chance threw us into each other's way, and I always felt a high regard for his upright and persevering character.

When the site at Saltaire opened on 20 September 1853, many provincial newspapers reported on the grand events. On 24 September, one such paper, the *Manchester Courier and Lancashire General Advertiser*, began their article on the proceedings by stating:

The most gigantic establishment that England possesses in the worsted trade was opened on Tuesday, amid much rejoicing, at Saltaire, a short distance from the rapidly improving manufacturing village of Shipley, about 3 miles from Bradford, situate upon the stream of the

Joseph Jackson's warehouse, King Street.

river Aire, which here gives its name to one of the most beautiful valleys that the West Riding of Yorkshire possesses.

The paper went on to praise the selection of the site, it being high in the valley, with a stream close by, 'unpolluted by the admixture of refuse from dye works.' The operation was described by the *Bradford Observer* as comprising buildings occupying 6 acres, with 'several floors of the mills, warehouses and sheds' taking this to over 11 acres, and the walls of 'massive stone' looking more like a fortified town than 'a building destined to the peaceful pursuits of commerce'.

So whilst it's unlikely that Wakefield was ever considered suitable for Sir Titus Salt's needs, perhaps the odd opportunity did slip through the grasp of the area in and around Kirkgate. But hindsight is a wonderful thing, and who knows whether crowds would have continued to flock to the bathhouse at New Wells. It's doubtful they would have come in the sort of numbers that are visiting one of the city's most recent ventures, the Hepworth Wakefield art gallery, which opened in 2011. Despite dissenting voices criticizing the scheme, citing the £18 million or so that it has received in investment from the council, it has proved a popular attraction, with half a million visitors striding through its doors in its first year. However, for all the pomp, the building itself was not met with universal enthusiasm from the local population. It earned the derisory moniker, 'Peter's Box', a reference to the building's appearance as something of a brutal eyesore, and the leader of Wakefield Council, Peter Box, who admitted to the BBC that 'some people don't like the building … they think it looks like a concrete bunker.' The concession from the leader of the council notwithstanding, the venue was awarded the Regional Building Award for 2012 by the Royal Institute of British Architects.

At the time of its opening, Peter Box also told the BBC that he hoped visitors would be 'blown away' by the quality of the exhibits, and that it would help to facilitate the regeneration of the area around the riverside. This is proving a slow process, but the gallery itself is certainly a local and national talking point, and the nearest station, Kirkgate, has undergone a major makeover. A restored station building was opened on 14 September 2015, following years of campaigning by the likes of local MP, Mary Creagh, and having once been declared (by Labour's then Secretary of State for Transport, Lord Adonis) as the worst of its size in Britain. Perhaps the station, with its new life breathed into it, might revive the days when the Topographical Society were conveyed to the town in style via the station to admire the likes of the Six Chimneys and the Chantry Chapel.

The Hepworth, Wakefield.

Kirkgate Station revamped.

Chapter Four

Warrengate

Further up Kirkgate, at the junction where the Six Chimneys public house and the former New Dolphin Inn stand, is Lower Warrengate, or Wrengate, as it used to be known.

It was once home to property belonging to the Manor of Newland. The centre of the manor, at Altofts, in the parish of Normanton (a few miles outside Wakefield), was the site of a preceptory of the religious order, the Knights Templar. The order at Newland was founded by King John in 1213, before the Knights Hospitaller, another Roman Catholic military order, took over by 1256. For almost 300 years the Knights Hospitaller remained at Newland, owning what E.W. Crossley, writing in the *Yorkshire Archaeological Society Record Series* volume 61 (published in 1920), described as 'numerous detached properties scattered over a large area of the West Riding of Yorkshire, Nottinghamshire, Cumberland, Westmorland and North Lancashire'. The properties

A cottage at Warrengate marked by the Newland Cross, denoting ownership by the Knights Hospitaller of Newland. *By courtesy of YAHS.*

were let, the leases affording the tenants certain privileges, including freedom from the Soke. Directly above 'Wrengate', on the 1851 Ordnance Survey map, the following note is recorded: 'Part of the Possessions of the dissolved Priory of the Knights of St John at Jerusalem and free of the Wakefield Soke.' Manorial income was derived from the rent on these properties and the farms attached to them, a notable lord of the manor, and preceptor being William Levett.

Ministers' Accounts from Newland, for 1539 and 1540 (reproduced by Crossley), contain the following entries:

> Wakefield. xvjd. [sixteen pence] from Wm. Dey for rent of one cottage with garden now in tenure of Alice Flathere.
>   iijs. [three shillings] from heirs of John Lake for rent of one mess. with croft adjoining Wrengate new built.

The order at Newland continued until the time of the dissolution, when the property was confiscated by Henry VIII. The preceptory was dissolved on 18 November 1540 and its preceptor pensioned off. Although revived by Queen Mary, who appointed Sir Cuthbert Layton as commander of Newland, the order never recovered.

In 1544 the site was sold to Francis and Elizabeth Jobson and others. The Jobsons conveyed the manor to Newton couple Richard Bunny and his wife Bridget in 1546 for a fee of £466 13s. 4d. and it passed to their heirs until it was sold again in 1694 to the Silvester family. The customs of the manor continued, though, as the will of Snydale yeoman Robert Fenton testifies. The will was proved at the Exchequer Court in York in 1762, and the original probate file is held at the Borthwick Institute for Archives at the University of York:

> I give and devise all my copyhold messuages, Lands Tenements and Hereditaments whatsoever situate lying and being at Snydall aforesaid or elsewhere in the County of York which I have heretofore surrendered to such uses as shall be declared by my last will & Testament to my Brother John Fenton and his Heirs forever according to the Custom of the Manor of Newland.

Robert had no issue, and whilst copyhold land could in theory be inherited, depending on the customs of a given manor, it is likely he held the land for life, with his brother John next in line to become the tenant. This was known as copyhold for lives, whereby three named persons would have an interest in the land. This would be the tenant and then two others.

When the tenant died the copyhold would pass to the next in line, in this case John Fenton. He would then name another person who would effectively go to the back of the queue. This predetermination meant that copyhold land did not often appear in wills, so Robert's bequest is interesting. The transfer of the land would have been entered in the court rolls of the manor, and this was known as an admission and surrender. Proof of the exchange would be given to the new tenant, John Fenton, in the form of a copy of the transfer. The tenant then held this copy, hence the term copyhold, and with this he could thereby prove his entitlement to the land, as tenant. The lord of the manor of Newland, an office that in 1762 was held by John Silvester Smith, retained overall possession of Fenton's land until such time that it became freehold.

It was John Silvester Smith's father, John Smith, who, in the early 1740s, built an impressive mansion on the estate called Newland Hall. This stood until it was razed to the ground in 1917 by then owners, William Locke and John Warrington, who had bought the estate in the 1860s and opened St John's Colliery on it in 1870. Throughout the 1870s, Locke lived at Sutton Hall in Sutton-on-the-Forest in the North Riding, and during this period, he offered Newland Hall for let. An advert for the lease appeared in the *Leeds Mercury* of 13 April 1872.

> To be LET, on Lease, within 10 miles of Leeds, three of Wakefield, and one-and-a-half of the Normanton Station, that capital FAMILY MANSION, Newland Hall, standing in a well-timbered park of about 60 acres, with walled gardens, greenhouse, vineries, peach house &c., pleasure grounds, and 18 acres of grass land. The hall comprises spacious entrance hall, lofty dining and drawing rooms, library, morning room, and study, nine principal bed rooms, with dressing rooms, six servants' rooms, housekeeper's room, servants' hall, butler's pantry, capital kitchen, scullery, dairy, laundry, and other offices, with excellent stabling, loose boxes, coach houses, all in good order. The hall is well supplied with water and lighted with gas. For all particulars apply at Hindle's Leeds and County Estate Offices, 23, Park-row.

It was advertised again in 1879, with a rather more curt notice offering immediate possession of the 'capital mansion', before William Locke and his family took up residency themselves by the time the 1881 census was compiled.

Newland Hall featured in the *Leeds Times* on 10 March 1888. The newspaper was reporting a round-up of news from Wakefield when the following story appeared:

SINGULAR CONDUCT OF A JOINER

> At Wakefield yesterday, William Henry Robinson, joiner and undertaker, of Altofts, was charged with having been on enclosed premises for an unlawful purpose. It appeared that on the 28th ult. Prisoner, about eight o'clock in the morning, rushed into Newland Hall, upstairs, and fastened himself in a bed-room, where he stayed some time. He was at length induced to emerge, and said two men had wanted to kill him. He was trembling violently and made a number of rambling statements. It appeared that he had had some money left and had been drinking hard lately, and was bound over to be of good behaviour for six months.

Though the estate was sold in 1926 to The Warmfield Company Limited, a brickmaking firm, the colliery continued to operate. The manager, and also the company secretary, lived in houses built out of the surviving stable block (otherwise known as the coach house). The manager's widow remained on the estate until 1959, following the death of her husband in 1946.

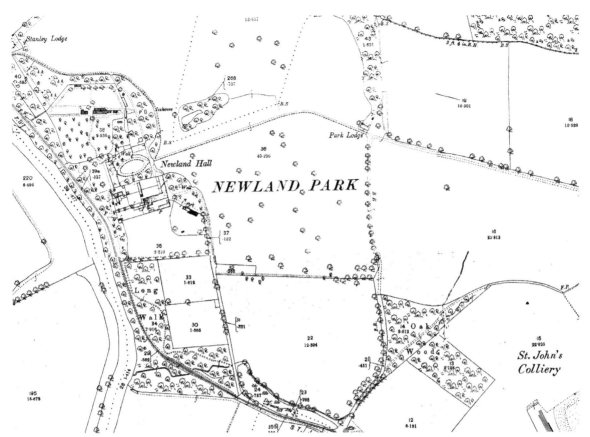

An Ordnance Survey map of 1892 (1:2,500) showing the Newland estate. St John's Colliery workings are to the right (just out of the frame) and St John's Colliery Railway emerges at the bottom of the image. Note the icehouse shown towards the top left, below Stanley Lodge. Along with Park Lodge, to the right of Newland Hall, there was also Old Lodge situated to the south-east of the hall. *By courtesy of old-maps.co.uk and Ordnance Survey.*

Some farm buildings, the ruins of a house built in 1935, and remnants of the hall's stable block can still be seen at the site today, and what remains has been awarded listed status. But a modern visitor seeking evidence of the preceptory, or indeed the grand old hall, will leave disappointed, if not a little spooked by the eerie way in which this once thriving estate has been despoiled.

During the Civil War, Royalist Wakefield was under the command of General Goring, who had assembled a garrison of 3,000 men, but on 21 May 1643 it was captured by Sir Thomas Fairfax's Parliamentary forces. The assault on the town was carried out at two points: Northgate and Warrengate, where Royalist barricades stood, and the operation was well timed. The day before the town's capture, General Goring and several other senior officers were enjoying a leisurely game of bowls on the green at Dame Mary Bolles' Heath Hall (later, Heath Old Hall), where guests were always well looked after. It was a warm Saturday afternoon, and after each bowl of a ball, alcoholic drinks were taken. Egged on by their commanding officer, it wasn't long before the merry company were roaring drunk. This was perhaps unsurprising, given that Goring had gained

Heath Old Hall. *By courtesy of YAHS.*

something of a notorious reputation as a bad-mannered man of ill habits. And following the Siege of Portsmouth in 1642, another town under his command, he was dubbed something of a coward after surrendering the town.

With Goring now lying sick from drink in his bed, unable even to make his head stop pounding, let alone command his troops, and word of the Royalists' antics having reached Fairfax, the Parliamentarian leader was presented with the perfect opportunity to strike. What was initially planned as a night raid took place early the next morning on Whitsunday, and the Parliamentarians were confident of success. It was just after one o'clock in the morning when Fairfax's troops, about 1,500 in number, assembled at Lord Savile's Howley Hall in Batley and began their march to Wakefield. Walker described part of their journey:

About half-past three o'clock Fairfax's army came up Stanley hill and to their surprise stumbled upon two troops of musketeers who lined the hedges in the fields known as 'the Cannonry' between the old bar and the top of Stanley hill, and the Little Gun croft in Stanley Park to defend

Another view of Heath Old Hall. *By courtesy of YAHS.*

a lane that in those days ran from the bottom of Stanley hill to join the lane at St Swithun's, and the Great Gun croft between Clarke Hall and the main road, which was guarded by a squadron of dragoons.

Walker cited the testimony of a Parliamentary officer named Lisle, who said that the men were 'beate … out of the hedges … where after six times charging we gat the hedges there, as others of our foote did in other places, and we gard them run fro us, and we took neither mare nor less than ane and twenty prisoners, and laid foure asleep for evermore.' By this time, Lisle said that the lark had begun to sing and Wakefield was but a mile away. It was four o'clock in the morning now and the approaching men discerned a 'body of Horse advancing with speed' towards them, which 'scard us mickle.' But cajoled by Fairfax, the mounted soldiers charged towards the Royalists, forcing them back towards the town, and at the same time more musketeers who 'lined the hedges along Eastmoor' were forced out of their hiding places, retreating to trenches dug in the town itself.

The Earl of Newcastle had given the Royalists four large brass guns with which to defend the town. It was Newcastle who had appointed Goring and had selected Wakefield, for its central location in the north, as an ideal place to store ammunition. One of these guns, however, was quickly captured, which, according to Lisle, elicited a cry of 'Walloway all was tint and gone!' from the Wakefield force. Walker also explained that Parliamentarian foot soldiers, under the command of Major General John Gifford, entered the town at Warrengate and 'seized the enemy's guns.' These had been positioned in the market place close to where Fairfax had charged the barricades at Northgate, as 'thick volleys of great and small shot' rained down on his forces.

The commotion finally roused Goring and he swiftly resolved to try to defend the town. Ignoring the terrible sickness brought on by all the alcohol taken at Heath the previous day, he galloped up Northgate to face the Parliamentarians, who'd been surprised to discover so many Royalists manning the town, when they'd expected to find so few.

What happened next, as Goring bore down on Fairfax's troops, was described in a letter written to the Speaker of the House of Commons by Lord Ferdinando Fairfax, a Parliamentary Leader (and also father of Sir Thomas Fairfax). The document was cited in volume XII of *Parliamentary or Constitutional History of England*, and it read:

upon Saturday last, in the Night, I caused to be drawn out of the Garrisons in Leeds, Bradford, Halifax, and Howley, some Horse, Foot, and Dragooners, in all about 1,500 Men, and sent them against Wakefield, commanded by my Son, and assisted by Major General Gifford, Sir Henry Fowlis, and Sir William Fairfax, with divers other Commanders: They appeared before Wakefield about Four o' Clock on Sunday in the Morning, where they found the Enemy, who had Intelligence of their Design, ready to receive them; there was in the Town General Goring, Serjeant Major General Mackworth, the Lord Goring, with many other principal Commanders and eminent Persons, about seven Troops of Horse, and six Regiments containing 3,000 Foot; the Town well fortified with Works, and four Pieces of Ordnance; yet our Men, both Commanders and common Soldiers, went on with undaunted Courage; and, notwithstanding the thick Vollies of small and great shot from the Enemies, charged up to their Works, which they entered, seized upon their Ordnance, and turned them upon themselves; and pursued the Enemy so close as they beat quite out of the Town the most Part of the Horse, and a great Number of the Foot, and made all the rest Prisoners; with them they took four Pieces of Ordnance, and all the Ammunition then in the Town, and a great Number of Arms; and, amongst the Prisoners, General Goring himself, with divers other commanders and other common Soldiers … I do rather account it a Miracle than a Victory; and the Glory and Praise be ascribed to God that wrought it; in which, I hope, I derogate nothing from the Merits of the Commanders and Soldiers, who every Man, in his Place and Duty, shewed as much Courage and Resolution as could [be] expected from Men. When the Town was thus taken, they found their Number and Strength too weak to keep it and their Prisoners, so left the Place and marched away with their Booty. In taking the Town we lost no Man of Note, and only seven Men in all; of which one was the Clerk of the Stores, an Ensign of Foot, and one Quarter-master of Horse, the rest common Soldiers; but many of our Men were shot and wounded. This Overthrow hath much enraged the Enemy, who threaten a present Revenge, and are drawing their Forces this Way to effect it.

Whilst the 1643 siege didn't quite signal the end of Royalist Wakefield, the town eventually fell lock, stock and barrel to the Parliamentarians on 1 October 1645, when the ramshackle Sandal Castle, thrice besieged during the conflict, was surrendered, before being put out of use completely by cannonball fire. It was at this time when the original monument to Richard, Duke of York, was said to have been removed, and that August a ferocious plague broke out that blighted the town for a year. Walker reckoned that during the months of August and September, 'the air was so warm and infectious that dogs, cats, mice, and rats died, and that several birds dropped down dead in their flight over the town.'

Sandal Castle ruins before extensive work was carried out to improve the site. *By courtesy of YAHS.*

Sandal Castle in 2015, with the lake at Pugney's Country Park shown on the left.

The ruins of the castle, still standing today as a relic of a time when the country went to war against itself, eventually drew in crowds of picnickers, ramblers and pleasure seekers.

The noted artist, Samuel Buck, drew a romanticized version of the ruins in 1722, and the vivid colours of the original print bring to life the distant prospect of the town, with the spire of the parish church as the centrepiece. It was at the church where those who died during the capture of the town in 1643 were buried. According to the church registers, held by West Yorkshire Archive Service, on 21 May 1643 there were '30 souldiers buried', followed by burials on 22 May of '4 souldiers'. Two entries on 4 July read: 'a souldier, a souldier'; two further burials of soldiers were noted on 6 July, and the following day an entry read: 'a souldier buried', confirming Walker's theory that some of the wounded 'lingered'. The registers also record burials of soldiers the following year. On 5 June 1644, two were buried, and on 7 June, the body of 'John Curbutt a souldier' was laid to rest.

Walker explained that thirty-five skeletons were discovered during work on the eastern extension of the church, which was completed in 1905. He said that 'the bodies had been laid in a long line, head and feet alternately, only a few feet below the surface of the ground near the boundary wall on the north side.' He assured his readers that the bones were reinterred 'within a few paces of the present vestry door of the Cathedral'.

It seems that in July 1903, just like on Whitsun 1643, Warrengate was a place best avoided. The *Yorkshire Evening Post* reported that an 'exciting arrest' had been made at Wakefield. The headline told how a 'man armed with a hatchet' defied the police, and that the 'fire hose' was 'brought into play'.

There was an exciting scene in Warrengate, Wakefield, about noon to-day. At the City Court during the morning a warrant was issued for the arrest of a man named William Stringer, a joiner, of Warrengate, on a charge of assaulting Betsy Moorhouse, a woman with whom he has lived for some thirty years.

Detective-officer Bell went to the house with the view of executing the warrant. He was met by Stringer, who is said to have been drinking heavily of late. Standing on the narrow staircase Stringer flourished a hatchet and threatened to kill anyone who went near him; and on Bell making a step forward he dealt him a severe blow on the head.

The assistance of other officers was obtained, but they had great difficulty in approaching Stringer, who armed himself with all the tools of a joiner's chest.

At last a hose cart was fetched from the fire station, and a stream of water was poured into the bedroom window. This did not, however, fetch Stringer out, and eventually the officers burst open the door of the room in which he had locked himself.

Stringer, thereupon tried to jump through the bedroom window, but the framework prevented him. He was then secured, but he had cut his head so badly in his attempt to get through the window that he had to be taken to the Clayton Hospital.

And in July 1905, Joe Hargrave's good friend, Mr Catterall, appeared in Wakefield City Court representing one Amy Murray, the complainant. Her husband, Joseph Murray, a cooper of Warrengate, was charged with attempting to murder her. Mr Catterall told the court that it seemed his client had 'no beneficial effect' on her husband, and Murray was remanded for a week. But before he was taken away, Mr Catterall announced he'd been in discussions with the chief constable, Murray's relatives and Murray himself. They'd decided between them that rather than detain Murray any further, he might like to try to turn over a new leaf somewhere aboard. When asked if there was anywhere in particular he fancied going, Murray replied that Canada sounded rather appealing!

A darker story emerged in July 1929, when reports appeared in the press of 'strange noises which told of a tragedy'.

It was a quarter to two in the morning on Monday, 15 July when local officer PC Dain heard some commotion coming from a house on Warrengate. When he went to investigate, he saw two youngsters banging on their bedroom window and shouting for help. On entering the house, at 21 Warrengate, he discovered the lifeless body of a 37-year-old lady named Mrs Winifred Pollard. Next to her, quite insensible, was her lover, John William Cock, a gasworks labourer, who was clinging to life. The pair were lying in the kitchen, covered in blood. It was quite apparent to the constable that they had terrible wounds to their necks. Cock lingered for two hours before dying in Clayton Hospital. The youngsters at the window were his children, Walter and Lily, and it fell to them to reveal what had happened.

An inquest into the deaths was held at Wakefield Town Hall, and the *Yorkshire Post* reported on the proceedings on 18 July 1929. Walter, aged eighteen, explained to the court that his father had been depressed, but that he was 'one of the best'. The children's mother, Annie, had died the previous year, and their older brother, Wilfred, had left home to join the army. To ease the sorrow these events had caused him, John William Cock had become friendly with a lady Walter knew only as Winnie.

Walter's sister, Lily, who was fourteen, described how on the night of the deaths she'd heard a noise from downstairs that sounded like her father quarrelling with somebody, but she'd soon drifted off to sleep again only to be woken later by a loud thud. She decided to take a look downstairs but as the gas was off she couldn't see anything, so returned to her bed. But not long after this, another sound awoke her so she went to get her brother. Lily then took a lighted candle downstairs and there discovered her father and Mrs Pollard lying on the floor, 'a pool of blood being between them.'

Lily recalled how, a week before the terrible events, her father had thrown Mrs Pollard out of the house for using 'awful' language, telling her plainly he never wanted to see her again. The young girl explained that Pollard had replied by telling her father, 'I shall get my own back; I shall do you in sometime.'

Cock had answered this by asking, 'What about my poor children?' to which Pollard said '---- your children.'

PC Dain said he'd attended the house after Walter and Lily had called for help, and on entering the kitchen he saw the bodies, immediately realizing that the female was dead, and the male unconscious. He found three pence in copper in the dead woman's hand, and a halfpenny lying on the hearth rug, but apart from a bloodstained razor, which PC Dain discovered on a table a few yards away, the house was otherwise 'in good order, and none of the furniture had been disarranged.'

Giving evidence, a Dr Robinson said that he did not believe that Pollard's wound was self-inflicted and it 'might have been done by the razor produced.' He surmised that Cock had probably caused his own injuries (he had cuts to his throat and to one of his wrists), before placing the razor down.

Cock's elder son, a private with the East Kent Regiment, put it to the doctor that perhaps Pollard had attacked first, and in defence his father had gone at her with the razor, cutting her throat before he threw away the blade. Dr Robinson supposed that in theory this was possible.

Winnie Pollard's illegitimate daughter, Mary Rayner, told the court that in 1919 her mother had married a man from Blackpool named William Pollard, but the couple had not lived together for the last six years. On Sunday, 14 July, the day before her death, Winnie had left her house on Sun Lane (which she and Mary shared with Elizabeth Rayner, Winifred's mother) at around twenty to ten in the evening to buy some beer. She never returned.

The inquest was adjourned until the following Tuesday (23 July), when Winnie Pollard's mother, Mrs Rayner, gave evidence. She told the inquest how her daughter had seemed agitated on that fateful Sunday morning because John had refused to take her out that evening. Winnie had remarked that 'that old devil is not going out tonight, but that will not stop me!' Mrs Rayner added that Winnie had also said that she didn't know 'what was the matter with the old devil'. The old woman confirmed that later that evening, Winnie had gone out to get some beer and supper. The coroner asked if she'd expected her daughter to move in with John Cock. To this Mrs Rayner said that she'd told Winnie that if she ever did, 'she had never to enter my door again.'

Mrs Rayner also told the coroner that Cock had threatened her daughter some six or seven weeks ago, telling he'd 'do her in'.

'He went white as sheet when he was annoyed,' Mrs Rayner continued, though she didn't know why this particular threat had been made.

Next, the coroner asked whether Winnie had a violent temper, to which Mrs Rayner answered: 'Yes, she had, but she was alright the next minute.' Her evidence was concluded when she told the coroner that her daughter had not been in gainful employment for quite some time.

A neighbour of Cock's, Elizabeth Hackett, said she'd seen Walter and Lily Cock returning home at around ten in the evening that Sunday. Hackett was enjoying the warm evening and stayed by

Warrengate and the Springs in the late nineteenth century. *By courtesy of YAHS.*

Warrengate and the Springs today.

her back door until just before midnight. During that time she'd seen Winnie, who was carrying a jug of beer, in conversation with Cock. Around twenty minutes after ten, Winnie was seen to enter Cock's house, and she had not left it by the time Hackett decided to turn in. At no point, Hackett claimed, had she'd heard any commotion from inside the house.

Despite Cock stating 'She did it!' as he lay dying in hospital, the jury, having listened to the evidence of Doctors Robinson and Sutherland, the latter attached to the County Medical Officer's Department, did not need long to conclude that Cock had inflicted both wounds. There was some suggestion that the razor couldn't have belonged to Cock as it had a white handle, and his, which he'd had for years, had a black handle. Nevertheless, the foreman of the jury, an ex-police sergeant, was quite clear in returning the verdicts. Cock, who was forty-nine, was found to have committed Winifred Pollard's murder, before fatally wounding himself.

On 12 October 1929, administration of John William Cock's estate was granted to Emily Rose Sale, the deceased's daughter, and Private Cock of East Kent Regiment. John William had left effects valued at £134 6s.

Present-day Warrengate is home to Sun Lane Leisure, the popular swimming baths and gymnasium, and an array of boutique shops where pooches can be pampered and brides-to-be bedecked in elegance. There's also a hotel, and a little further up the road is the Trinity Walk shopping complex.

Sun Lane Leisure.

Trinity Walk shown from Vicarage Street, just off Warrengate.

Chapter Five

Westgate, beyond, and back again

Anybody going down to Mr Haselgrave's Zoological Gardens in the grounds of the Orangery on Saturday, 1 June 1844 would have been sure of a big surprise.

The Orangery, which stands on Back Lane, is adjacent to the new Westgate Station. It was formerly a distant backdrop to the now defunct station of the same name. The grounds, a recent venue for music and literary festivals, formed a garden for cloth merchant Pemberton Milnes, whose Pemberton House, at 122 Westgate, stood by the entrance to the old station. Pemberton Milnes died in 1795 and the property came into the hands of his daughter, Dowager Vicountess Galway. She had the Orangery erected shortly after the site came into her hands.

In 1835, following Lady Galway's death, aged eighty-two, and her subsequent burial within the catacombs of Westgate Unitarian Chapel, where she rests bedecked in her finest jewels, the site was offered for sale. As reported in the *Leeds Times*, on 20 October 1838, the location attracted the attention of Thomas Haselgrave, a seed and hop merchant of Wakefield. He hoped to open zoological gardens there, which were becoming popular across the country: such an attraction had opened at Sheffield in 1836, followed by another at Headingley in 1840.

ZOOLOGICAL GARDEN AT WAKEFIELD

We lately mentioned that Mr Haselgrave, of Wakefield, seed and hop merchant, was projecting a Zoological Garden. Workmen are now employed in undulating the building, forming pleasant retreats, paddocks for various animals, erecting imitation rocks, sinking ponds, digging bear-pits, and raising an orchestra. The green-houses and hot-houses are made subsidiary to the design. The prospectus will be advertised in due time, and we have no doubt the public will patronize the project with becoming spirit.

Some months later, and while the site was still being prepared, the Wakefield Floral Society were allowed to hold their annual tulip show in the gardens. The event was described in the *Leeds Times* of 8 June 1839 as being 'the best that has ever taken place in Wakefield both as to the quantity and quality of the flowers'. The interior of the building was, according to the paper, 'elegantly decorated with tastefully arranged bouquets', and it was hoped that 'the spirited proprietor, Mr Haselgrave, will not be suffered to lose in his attempt to afford a rational and gratifying source of amusement.'

Later that month, notices appeared in provincial newspapers announcing that Mr Haselgrave's 'Botanical and Zoological Gardens' were to be 'furnished' with public baths, the *Leeds Times* announcing in July that the 'swimming bath in connection with the Botanical and Zoological Garden at Wakefield is now open to the public.' The paper was sure that 'the proprietor will be well encouraged.'

Thomas Haselgrave was a family man. He'd married twice, first to Elizabeth Coop in 1823, and then to Ann Coop, whom he wed in 1835, one month after Elizabeth's death. Both wives had borne him children, and they all were close to their aunt, Hannah. She'd married Thomas's brother, Joseph, at St John's Church on 1 August 1824, and in 1832 they had a daughter, Anna Maria, whom they baptised on Christmas Day the following year. Joseph died in his mid-forties in June 1838, and Hannah, who was living on Providence Street at this time, was left to bring up her daughter alone, though Thomas and Ann supported her.

In August 1839 it was reported that a floral competition would be held at the site in September, and anybody residing within the county was free to show their dahlias and carnations. This rule was changed to allow anybody in the country to descend on Wakefield with their offerings. Thomas Haselgrave himself made the papers soon afterwards, following his discovery of what was dubbed at the time, a 'remarkable onion', weighing 25 ounces.

The following year, the *York Herald* reported that Haselgrave had fallen victim to a 'daring robbery' when seven of his Spanish rabbits were taken late one Saturday night, or early the following morning, by a 'villain or villains' who entered the premises in Back Lane and made off with the valuable animals.

Then, on 2 January 1841, the *Leeds Times* announced the sudden death of one of Haselgrave's prized attractions, a well-known bear named Bruin, who performed for visitors and lived in the bear pit at Wakefield, having previously resided at Sheffield's Botanical Gardens.

SUDDEN DEATH OF BRUIN

On Tuesday last, at the Zoological Gardens, Wakefield, the celebrated bear Bruin, died from the prevalent epidemic among cattle. This ponderous animal was a native of America, and … could climb a pole 12 feet high, with amazing alacrity: its antics in fact were innumerable.

The acquisition of Bruin's successor would lead to a terrible tragedy that ultimately spelled the end for the 'spirited' Thomas Haselgrave's endeavours. It would also lay bare the terrible cost of keeping animals without proper provision for their safety, the safety of those in charge of them, and of those merely coming to gawp.

One such example of maltreatment leading to dire consequences was reported in the 23 December 1843 edition of the *Sheffield Iris*, when the newspaper told its readers that the elephant kept at the Sheffield zoological gardens had 'offended one of the deputy keepers'. The elephant had just finished entertaining a group of young visitors with one of his 'majestic performances' when the deputy keeper took to beating him with a broom handle. What happened next was unclear, but within a few moments 'the keeper was found lying at the feet of the insulted beast, with his face to the ground, perfectly lifeless.'

On Saturday, 1 June 1844, Thomas Haselgrave was away from home attending to some business or other, and had left the gardens in the charge of his wife, Ann, and his sister-in-law, Hannah, who was now living in Back Lane. It was about eight o'clock in the morning; the replacement bear, who was reckoned to be about three years of age, was in her pit and the grounds were ready to be opened for the day.

A young biscuit seller named Joseph Gledhill, fancying his chances at selling his wares to the Haselgraves, had called at the house. Before going in, he decided to take a walk around the grounds. As he passed the bear pit, he stopped to observe the occupant. Though he later swore to the contrary, it was believed the lad took a biscuit from his pocket and began teasing the bear with it, offering it to her and then withdrawing it just as she came within reach. Just as Joseph's game was beginning to amuse him, the bear leapt out from the pit, 'making a noise, and springing about the place.' The boy watched on in frozen horror as the creature dragged herself to ground level, facing him eye to eye. Coming to his senses, Joseph sprang to life and dashed into the house. He cried for Mr Haselgrave's elder daughter, Ann.

'The bear's got out; the bear's got out!'

Mr Haselgrave's wife heard the cries and witnessed the escape. She came downstairs and prepared to go outside to try to drive the bear back into her pit. Not daring to face the animal on her own, she called for Hannah, who answered the call. The younger of the Anns joined the rescue party, and armed with a brush and some of Joseph's biscuits, they hoped they could coax her back to her dwelling. Young Ann approached cautiously, but the bear charged at her, so she ditched the brush and ran to safety.

Confused and agitated by all the fuss, the bear picked up the brush and played with it for a few moments, before Hannah approached and beat her with a stick. Defending herself, the bear attacked the widow, knocking her to the ground. Ann senior picked up a stick of her own and struck the creature at least three times. With a fourth swing of the stick, Ann managed to bring the weapon down on the bear's head, but this only worsened the situation and Ann was seized, as screams echoed around the pleasure gardens.

As Hannah managed to free her sister-in-law from the bear's grasp, the animal sunk its claws into her back and turned her over. Ann was wounded and pouring with blood, and could do nothing more to help. At this point, her daughter ran out of the grounds and on to Back Lane, crying for help. There she saw Mr Stead, a local druggist, who was dashing to the scene. His house overlooked the gardens and his wife had heard the blood-curdling cries of the women and urged him to help. He'd grabbed a garden hoe and headed for the calamity. He found that his hoe made a barely effective weapon, his thrusting of it only causing the creature to turn on him.

The distraction enabled Hannah to get away, and she headed for the gate below the house. But it was no good. The bear caught up with her and tore at her breast with its forepaws.

Mr Stead found shelter in an outbuilding, to where he'd retreated in order to recover his breath. Looking out of a dirty window, he saw that his father had arrived and was conveying Hannah to the house, her terrible injuries clearly visible.

More assistance was soon at hand. Broughton Boston, son of Mr Boston, the gun maker, William Drake, local plumber and glazier, and Thomas Hudson, a servant to a local doctor, had all come to see what help they could offer. Mr Drake had been working at the nearby prison when he too had heard the screams, and had seen old Mr Stead making his way to the gardens. Drake and Boston were armed with guns, and the arrival of these three men distracted the bear. Growling and whining, she headed straight for them. Drake fired first, but he was too far away and the charge did no serious harm to the bear. Boston, on the other hand, knew how to fire his father's guns and he stalked the bear, looking for the optimum spot from where to fire at her. Reaching the lower part of the garden, he found he was able to get within 2 yards of his target and promptly blasted her in the head, causing the animal to roll over in shock and pain. He took a step back, reloaded and sent the bear from this world.

The garden was soon full of several more armed parties, hatchets and pistols just some of the weapons on show, but these were not needed. In spite of this, it did not stop some latecomers claiming to have saved the day.

But the day was not saved for Hannah. She was treated by Dr Wood and a Mr Burrell, but her left arm was soon found to be beyond repair, and her legs and thighs were lacerated severely. She lingered for several days, but succumbed to her injuries, dying on 9 June, aged fifty-three. The following day she was buried at St John's Church, following a service conducted by Reverend Kilby, the minister-cum-artist. Ann Haselgrave, Thomas's wife, survived the attack.

The inquest into Hannah Haselgrave's death was held on the day of her burial at the Black Horse Inn, just yards from the fateful scene. It was conducted by the coroner, Thomas Lee, who found that, despite the boy's claim to the contrary, Joseph Gledhill had been in the habit of giving the bear biscuits, though Gledhill swore he hadn't been teasing the animal on the day. It was also discovered that the creature, who had been bought by Thomas Haselgrave in Leeds a couple of years earlier, had escaped before, just a few weeks prior to the dreadful incident. Instead of digging a deeper pit, which the coroner suggested might have prevented the tragedy, a higher wall had been erected, Thomas Haselgrave insisting that his pit was deeper even than the bear pit at the Paris Zoological Gardens.

Haselgrave maintained that the bear was not prone to attacking anybody, and it was also heard that Hannah Haselgrave wasn't afraid of the creature, telling the family to call on her any time if there was a problem with it. Crucially, though, the two females had only ever stood and watched the bear; they'd never played any part in its care. One rumour flying about the town had suggested the bear attacked the women because it was hungry, though young Ann Haselgrave told the inquest that her father had assured her he had fed the bear before he set off at around seven that morning. She'd been instructed to throw something into the pit in the afternoon.

At the conclusion of the inquest, a verdict of accidental death was returned.

Just two months after the death of Hannah Haselgrave, a curious report appeared in the *Leeds Mercury*:

WILFUL DAMAGE

On Tuesday last, a man named Thomas Haselgrave was ordered by the magistrates at the Leeds Court House, to pay 30s. and costs, or in default to go to Wakefield for six weeks, for having been drunk on Monday night, and whilst in that state broken thirteen squares of glass in a window belonging to Mr Lengthorn, the Brown Bear Inn, Kirkgate [in Leeds].

Of course, going to Wakefield for six weeks was a reference to the threat of a spell inside the prison there; but was this the same Thomas Haselgrave of Back Lane? It is perhaps tempting to imagine poor Thomas, lamenting the inevitable downturn in fortunes he was about to face – his visitors too frightened to patronize his gardens anymore – passing the aforementioned public house as he drowned his sorrows, noting the name of the establishment, and in a fit of bitterness, smashing its windows to smithereens.

The Haselgraves moved to Leeds soon after this, Thomas, now decidedly dispirited, having giving up his interest in botany and zoology. As for Ann, his wife, she died in Leeds in 1850, though Thomas would live for another twenty years, working as gardener. He'd see his children married,

The Orangery from Back Lane, showing the Horner monument.

Back Lane, by Henry Clarke. *By courtesy of WLSL.*

including young Ann, the daughter who'd witnessed the entire sorry event at the Orangery. She married carrier Henry Kirkbride in 1856 at St Peter's Church (now Leeds Minster), having lived with her father, and brother James, at Claremont Place and Rockingham Street.

The Orangery and grounds were eventually sold to Daniel Gaskell, Liberal Member of Parliament for Wakefield from 1832 to 1837. In 1850, Gaskell passed the site to the trustees of the adjacent chapel where Lady Galway had been buried, and since then the building has been used for various purposes. Worshippers at the chapel used it as a Sunday school, the children conveyed from chapel to school via an underground tunnel, which also acted as a passage for coffins when the ground became a graveyard. Headstones can still be seen in the gardens, along with a broken column commemorating the life of Joseph Horner junior, son of the corn miller who performed penance at the parish church in 1850. Joseph junior died aged thirty-seven, just a few months after the sorry episode involving his father, when he gave a spirited address to the gathered crowds. He was an important figure in the history of the Chartist movement, the inscription upon the Orangery monument praising his 'consistent advocacy of religious, moral, social and political rights and liberties for the people'.

In more recent times, the Orangery has been used as an arts venue, under the management of a company named Beam, hosting various events and festivals, though this ceased in 2015, and its future is now uncertain.

Just a short walk from Back Lane is the junction with Love Lane, the site of the formidable Her Majesty's Prison Wakefield, a jail housing Category A prisoners. Formerly known as the West Riding House of Correction, the original prison was erected in 1595, and partly funded by a sum of £20 left in the will of Wakefield benefactor, George Savile. His estate was proved at York on 17 February 1594–95. The relevant extract from the will reads:

Also I give twentie poundes for and towardes the buildinge of an House of Correction within seaven miles of Wakefield for the setting of the poore on worke or towardes a stocke for the keepinge of them in worke according to the statute if so be there any such house builded within the space of two yeres next after my decease and if there be not then this bequest utterlie to be void.

Savile, or 'Savill' as his name was written in the will, was a gentleman of Wakefield who had also provided funds in his will 'to the governors of the schole of Queen Elizabeth at Wakefield' in order to endow the establishment, which still stands on Brook Street (then known as Goody Bower).

The original house of correction is long gone, and information about it is scant, though records show further building work took place early in the century following its erection. In his book, *The Annals of Wakefield House of Correction*, published in 1904, Horsfall-Turner stated that it stood at the bottom of Westgate, the site in his day forming part of the women's prison. The likeliest

The Elizabethan Grammar School, by Henry Clarke. *By courtesy of WLSL.*

Savile inscriptions on the
Elizabeth Grammar School.
By courtesy of YAHS.

The site today.

The site of Wakefield House of Correction.

location is marked by a Wakefield Civic Society blue plaque, which was installed in 2000 at the corner of Westgate End and Back Lane on a wall in front of a prison building, the site of which, according to nineteenth-century Ordnance Survey maps, was used as 'Females Apartments'.

Following a successful escape attempt by one of the prisoners, it was decided that the jail was outdated and unfit for purpose. A new building was erected in the latter part of the 1760s, construction overseen by eminent Horbury-born architect, John Carr. Much of today's prison was built, as another brand-new facility, in 1847. Almost 170 years on, the building still serves its intended purpose, standing testament to Victorian durability.

In all of the prison's history, there have been several disturbances, numerous escapes, some failed attempts at liberation, and even conspiracies to break inmates out.

In April 1740, reports emerged of public disturbances at Dewsbury, Batley, Earls Heaton and other nearby villages. The trouble spread to Wakefield the following weekend, and would culminate in events involving the prison. The unrest had broken out when inhabitants of these places became determined to stop local badgers (dealers in food) producing wheat meal and flour for sale outside of Yorkshire, as they feared this would increase the price of corn locally.

Towards the end of the month, 500 people gathered and headed for Dewsbury Mill. On the way, they passed a cart belonging to a mill owner named John Wilson. Thinking it was loaded with flour, they attacked the cart, only to discover that Wilson had received word of their plans and had filled his sacks with dust instead. Deceived, the crowd went to his mill, where they smashed equipment and stole his meal.

A week later, the swelling mob repeated their actions at another mill in Dewsbury, prompting the High Sheriff, Sir Samuel Armytage, to take action, and he caused the Riot Act to be read. Hearing of the trouble, Sir John Kaye and his servants went to assist the High Sheriff. Refusing to disperse as ordered, the crowd instead took up stones and whatever other missiles they could lay their hands on and began flinging them at Kaye's men. When they finally grew tired, the mob marched to a mill at Thornhill, once more taking away meal and corn and destroying part of the building. Before they left, they also made off with the mill owner's beef and bacon.

A day later, expecting that the rioters would descend upon his house at Grange, Sir John Kaye, with the help of Sir Samuel Armytage, arranged for the local justices of the peace to meet there and hear the crowd's complaints. Now 1,000 strong, the crowd arrived as anticipated, beating drums, and yelling their defiance at the gathered officials. They didn't stay to talk, instead leaving to wreak havoc at Bretton, Woolley and Newmillerdam, their target being bolting mills (separate rooms at mills containing equipment used to sift grain to make it suitable for meal and flour).

Much like the Peasants' Revolt of 1381, numbers swelled as the Yorkshiremen passed through townships and parishes, supporters and hangers-on joining the cause as they progressed. Now within a few miles of Wakefield, the congregation arrived at Crigglestone in the parish of Sandal Magna. Here they broke into Joseph Pollard's barn, removing a vast quantity of the man's flour. However, they finally met with some real resistance, Pollard owning a small arsenal. He fired on the men and was able to take some prisoners, whom he conveyed to Wakefield Prison without haste.

Incensed, the rest of the mob continued marching towards Wakefield, where officials were holding urgent meetings to decide what on earth to do about the approaching tumult, the sound of beating drums signalling the mob's arrival. When they reached the town, at about two in the afternoon, the rioters stated their intentions. They'd come to demand the release of Pollard's prisoners, and if they weren't set free then the rioters promised to return to Pollard's house, pull it down, hang Pollard by a rope and skin him like a dead cat. Captain Burton, charged with seeing off the trouble, was having none of this, and he went to the head of the crowd where he proceeded to beat the ringleaders with a stick, knocking several to the ground. He took seven men prisoner and brought them to the House of Correction to join the others.

Later that day, soldiers from York arrived in Wakefield and took the prisoners back to York. The presence of the soldiers quickly brought the trouble to an end, though newspapers noted that there were still 'great murmurings among the Common People'.

On 29 March 1774, the *Leeds Intelligencer* reported that several of the prison's inmates had broken out. The report described their colourful appearances (for these were the days before Wakefield's prisoners sported uniforms) and the prices on each escapee's head.

BROKE out of the HOUSE of CORRECTION at Wakefield, on Friday Night the 18th February last, about Seven o' Clock in the Evening.

THOMAS HARRISON – Committed for paying counterfeit Bills, about thirty Years of Age, and about 5 Feet 10 Inches high, of a dark Complexion, had on when he broke out, a slouch'd Hat, brown cut Wig, dark-brown Coat, Metal Buttons, a Manchester Velvet Waistcoat, a Cinnamon coloured Surtout Coat, almost new, bound round, Buttons of the same Colour, Cluth Breeches, Colour of his Coat, blue and white mottl'd Stockings, strong Shoes, and Steel Buckles.

JAMES HARRISON – Committed for the same Offence, appears to be about twenty-six years of Age, about 5 Feet 5 Inches high, light-colour'd short Hair, fresh Complexion, a reddish Scar upon his right Cheek, Pock-broke, had on a shabby Hat, a Cinnamon-colour'd Surtout Coat, bound round, Buttons same Colour, dark-brown Coat, with yellow Metal Buttons, brown Waistcoat, with yellow Metal Buttons, dirty Leather Breeches, blue-grey worsted Stockings, turn'd Pumps, and plated Buckles.

WILLIAM SIMPSON – Committed for Felony, about twenty-five Years of Age, and about 5 Feet 8 Inches high, well made, brown lank Hair, Pock-broke, had on a good Hat, bound round with Velvet, Copper-colour'd Coat, Silver-plated Buttons, red spotted Waistcoat, Snuff-colour'd riding Coat, dirty Leather breeches, black stockings, Oval narrow Silver Buckles.

WILLIAM SCARGILL – Committed for Felony, about 5 Feet 7 Inches high, broad made, Pock-broke, fair Complexion, flaxen-colour'd bushy Hair, had on a slouch'd Hat, white Flannel Waistcoat, with Leather Buttons, dirty Leather Breeches, light-grey worsted Stockings, strong Shoes, plated Buckles.

THOMAS MASON – Committed on Suspicion of Felony, about 5 Feet 5 or 6 Inches high, black Complexion, Roman Nose, a Mole upon his left Jaw, a Scar upon his Forehead, another over his left Eye, had on a Macaroni Hat, dark-drab Thickset Coat, Buttons the same, blue-grey Waistcoat, lin'd with black, Metal Buttons, dirty Leather Breeches, and blue-great worsted Stockings.

RICHARD BROGDEN – Committed as a Deserter from the 37th Regiment of Foot, dark-brown short curl'd Hair, fresh-colour'd, a red Scar upon his Cheek, sharpish Nose, had on a blue Surtout Coat, double-breasted, yellow Metal Buttons, dirty Leather Breeches, clouted at the Knees, grey worsted Stockings.

Any Person securing the above-nam'd Persons, and delivering them up to John Waugh, the Keeper of the House of Correction in Wakefield, shall receive from the said Keeper, the following Rewards, viz.

For the two Harrisons, five Guineas each.

For Simpson, three Guineas.

For Scargill and Mason, two Guineas each.

For Brogden, one Guinea.

Such notices were not uncommon at this time, despite the new prison being built specifically for the purpose of preventing such escapes. In 1770, the same newspaper warned the public about one George Renton, alias Rodgers, an 18-year-old with an egg-shaped tattoo above his right eye, who was at large, having escaped from Wakefield on 1 December. William Hudson and John Martin, who'd both refused to pay for their illegitimate children, had also got out. There were two guineas on offer for the return of Renton, and a guinea each was the reward for the capture of Hudson and Martin.

Poor John Waugh, 'the keeper' of the house, put his name to a series of notices. A John Prockter escaped from custody in 1791, and once again the prisoner's colourful apparel ought to have helped bring about his capture. Prockter, a convicted burglar, who had a 'down look', was sporting a new woollen hat when he made free, an 'old shepherd grey coat' along with a red and white striped waistcoat. Bounties had increased over the years, and ten guineas were on offer in exchange for information pertaining to the whereabouts of Prockter.

In 1849, by which time inmates were dressed in standard prison clothing, the *Bradford Observer* printed the following story:

> The Late Escape from Wakefield Prison
> We understand the man who so dexterously escaped a few weeks since from Wakefield Prison, has sent a letter stating that he is thankful for the loan of the prison dress, and that he is now on the wide ocean, and the authorities may catch him if they can.

The story of the escape had been widely reported a month earlier. It occurred on the night of Sunday, 14 January. The faithful paper, the *Leeds Intelligencer*, was on top of the story, as were the *Durham County Advertiser* and *Reading Mercury*, to name just a few. At the time in question, the jail was being used to house prisoners awaiting transportation. One such prisoner, referred to as Smith, had been brought to Wakefield from Salisbury, having been sentenced to fourteen years' transportation for carrying out highway robberies. He was confined in C Wing in the new prison (which had opened in 1847), and had been learning how to weave. As a result of his interest in the trade, Smith had been provided with a loom, which was kept in his cell. As well as his loom he was also given a knife to cut his thread. But instead of putting it to legitimate use, Smith used this implement to remove the putty from the glass in his window, hiding it in his cell pan. Next, he took some tow from his loom (short fibres used for weaving into a coarser fabric) and wrapped it around the iron frame of his window until it was thick. He was then able, using a piece of machinery from his loom, to remove the window, which he did as quietly as he could. But before he departed through the newly created aperture, he fashioned himself a ladder from the strips of metal to which his loom was affixed to the cell wall. With his ladder under his arm, Smith crossed the yard and made for the outer wall, which he surmounted using the ladder, finding himself within the open fields that lay at the back of the prison. Nobody saw him escape, and though the night watchman had claimed to have made his half-hourly checks to ensure everybody was present, it was a few hours before anybody realized that Smith had gone.

Perhaps it was the outbreak of cholera at the prison that had prompted Smith to act. In January 1849, the disease caused the deaths of several inmates, and in some cases life expired within just a few hours of its onset. A joiner who was serving time was asked to make a coffin for one of the dead prisoners but no sooner had he completed his task, he too fell victim and was buried in his own creation. By the time the *Leeds Intelligencer* had gone to press on 27 January, there had been twenty-six cases, sixteen of which resulted in death.

On 12 October 1850, the *York Herald* ran the following headline: 'ESCAPE OF ANOTHER CONVICT FROM WAKEFIELD PRISON'. The story proclaimed that one of the 'most daring escapes from prison which the annals of our jail system have exhibited, has been performed during the last few days, by a convict confined in the prison at Wakefield.'

This time the escapee was a Boroughbridge watchmaker who'd been found guilty of highway robbery, his punishment being transportation for life. Prior to being transported, the prisoner was accommodated at Wakefield on the second tier of one of the newly built wings, and he spent his time making hammocks for which the prison allowed him the use of sticks 3 feet in length and just under an inch in diameter. He was also given vast quantities of bed-binding. He'd kept hold of a tool from his watchmaking profession, a small saw, which he concealed about his person. He used this to file down the bars of his cell window. Still sharp, the saw was used to remove the iron frame, before he took the glass out and waited for his opportunity. When the dawn of early morning was upon him, providing just enough light to bring about his escape, but still dark enough to ensure he wasn't seen, he jumped from the window, taking with him, just like Smith, a ladder fashioned from the hammock-making sticks, with the bed-binding holding the frame together. He used this to climb the same wall Smith had overcome, and he made off over the very same fields.

It wasn't only the male prisoners who were adept in the art of escaping. In March 1864, local papers reported that one Mary Ellen Renshaw, who was six months into a six-year sentence, had made it out of the jail. Finding her cell door unlocked, she simply walked out, carrying her 18-month-old child, with whom she was confined. As she passed the office of the prison matron, Mary Ann Abson, she discovered that the door was unlocked. Seizing her chance, Renshaw dressed herself in the matron's spare uniform, which she found hanging on the back of the door. To her continued good fortune, Renshaw also found that a set of keys had been left unattended. These allowed her to open door after door, and at last she found herself in the yard that led to the outer gate. The gatekeeper, seeing who he thought was Miss Abson in her familiar attire, straw bonnet and woollen shawl, thought nothing of allowing her out, the escaping prisoner even bidding him 'goodnight' as she walked by.

She was soon recaptured, and it appeared that Mary Ann Abson had colluded with Renshaw. At a hearing at the prison, Abson was duly charged with aiding Renshaw's escape. Renshaw told the hearing how she'd learned that Abson had stolen a shawl. The matron, fearing Renshaw would tell the governor, swore the convict to secrecy, keeping her quiet with regular supplies of bacon, tea, sugar and cheese. Abson also allowed Renshaw out of her cell at night. In the end, it seemed that Abson had decided it would be simpler just to let Renshaw escape. According to the prisoner,

Abson had left Renshaw's cell door unlocked and arranged for her to 'find' a silk dress, scarf, shawl, boots and a bonnet in her office. There, Abson instructed Renshaw to get changed and then walk calmly out of the gate.

The evidence seemed overwhelming, but at the Pontefract Sessions, held on 15 April, Mary Ann Abson was found not guilty of the charge against her, prompting much applause from the public gallery who were sympathetic to the matron and didn't believe a single word of Renshaw's story.

Tales of daring escapes persisted. In June 1890, a prisoner named Robert Hipps managed to pick the lock of his cell door, and going through another door, found he was able to access the roof. From there he used a waterspout as a slide, which conveyed him into the prison yard, from where he was able to jump from the upper floor of an empty building, over the prison wall, and run away through the well-trodden open fields.

Later that year, Arthur Williams, who had also escaped from the jail, having somehow fashioned a key to his cell door, was recaptured when he was arrested for stealing from a Rochester clothier. Williams had walked from Wakefield Prison all the way to the south of England, and was sentenced to a further seven years' imprisonment for the theft.

In 1914, a prisoner feigned sickness and then escaped from the hospital ward. A decade later, on Boxing Day 1924, a Halifax man named Harold Wheatley was jailed at Wakefield for shop-breaking, but not finding confinement to his liking, he simply climbed the high wall at night and made off. Having broken free, he went to Rufford Street, off Alverthorpe Road, where he found an empty house, the tenant away on his Christmas holidays. To disguise himself, he threw off his prison clothes and rifled through the wardrobe of the house, and according to the *Yorkshire Post*, took a liking to 'an overcoat, trousers, under-vest, cricket shirt, necktie, dinner jacket and vest, and a cap'. He even took the time to write 'Happy New Year!' in a notebook he'd found lying on the tenant's dining table before disappearing into the night. Wheatley was finally discovered in Newcastle in February 1925, and returned to prison.

In 1928 a convicted car thief, who had been entrusted to assist with alterations to the boundary walls outside of the prison, decided to absent himself, despite having only a few months of his sentence left to serve. As he was wearing overalls while working on the walls, he did not arouse suspicion in the city as he made his getaway.

January 1932 saw three men escape, though one was quickly recaptured just outside the prison. They'd been taking part in a gymnastics class, and finding the room to be poorly lit, and their warders momentarily distracted, they wandered off unseen. One of the men was recaptured the next day in Ossett following a violent scuffle after he was caught stealing cigarettes and chocolates.

Later that year, a prisoner who was working on an allotment with nineteen other inmates was able to make off in the direction of Alverthorpe, choosing to walk rather than run, as he presumably thought that beating a hasty retreat would arouse suspicion. He was recaptured after just a day, having returned to his native Mirfield, where he was soon recognized.

More and more stories of daring and brazen escapes filled the pages of the local newspapers, including one in 1946 when two men, a French polisher and a labourer, were thought to have

The Governor's House. *By courtesy of YAHS.*

disguised themselves in suits owned by the deputy governor, which they had stolen from his house (part of the prison buildings) while he was away on holiday. They were soon found following their arrests for breaking into a canteen at Dent Main Colliery in Middlesbrough in order to steal refreshments to sustain themselves while on the run.

In 1949, reports of a wild chase through the streets of Wakefield made the papers when an off duty prison officer, walking through Kirkgate, having just been to a cinema there, recognized two of his charges wandering about the city. With the help of passers-by, including an amateur boxer, he was able to detain them. The party chased them through Kirkgate, and eventually overpowered them at Eastmoor, where the boxer threw one of the men over a fence. They'd earlier made their escape from prison, climbing over a 30-foot wall with a third man who was found hiding in the garden at another prisoner officer's house.

These days it is far less likely that an inmate would be able to give prison officers the slip, and it's doubtful that looms and knives are handed out freely to the modern convicts of Wakefield Prison.

Escaping convicts of John Hewitt's day might have found themselves passing by the discarded burial ground at Westgate Common, just off Westgate End, had they taken Mary Ann Renshaw's route, straight out of the front gate.

At the bottom of Westgate End is the junction with Alverthorpe Road, formerly known as Humble Jumble Lane. A little further up is Kemp's Bridge, named after local doctor Benjamin Kemp. Over the bridge and beside the ruin of the old Westgate End House, for many years a doctor's surgery, was the site of Warburtons, the bread makers, and locals will well recall the strong aromas that wafted from the factory.

Demolished in recent years, the Warbutons site now stands empty; a baron wasteland, with no sign of the housing development that was mooted in Wakefield Council's Local Development Framework, which was adopted in April 2009.

Before bread was baked here, this place was once the site of a non-conformist meeting house, where Independents and Presbyterians gathered from 1697. These religious movements had gained a footing as a result of the 1662 Act of Uniformity, which led to non-conformists formally abandoning the Established Church. In the appendix of the published copies of the 1743 diocesan returns of Thomas Herring, Archbishop of York, it is noted that in 1715 the congregation was 400 strong, with forty of these being freehold property owners. However, as recent times have shown, Westgate End was not a practical site, owing to the effects of wet weather. Flooding at Chald beck, which flows past the site, eventually forced the congregation to retreat further

Old prison officers at Wakefield.

An old view of Wakefield Prison and surrounding fields.

Westgate End House, by Henry Clarke. This grand house was built on a large site with stables and coach houses. In 1953, a Dr Norton practised from here. The doctor amassed a huge collection of Irish books, maps and photographs, which he kept at the house. The Norton Collection is now held by the University of Limerick. *By courtesy of WLSL.*

up Westgate, where, in 1752, they opened a new chapel on the site of the current Unitarian Chapel. Though the congregants had moved to a new site, the use of the burial ground at Westgate End continued, and in 1862 John Hewitt paid a visit, conducting a sort of gravestone census, recording extant inscriptions and publishing them in one of the volumes of his scarce book.

Hewitt commented that:

Few people in the Parish of Wakefield know there is an old Grave-Yard on Westgate Common, in the township of Alverthorpe-with-Thornes; but such is the fact, for I have often visited this Presbyterian Burial-Ground, and if ever 'meditations amongst tombs' induced melancholy feelings to pervade the human breast, I am sure no more appropriate (if that term may be allowed) place could be gone to by the living to produce such painful feelings, or to muse upon the dead, than this abandoned Burial-Place. No internments now take place in it; but it still contains many Grave-Stones, with Inscriptions upon them.

In the entry for 'Warburtons, Westgate End' in the Local Development Framework, the council remarked that 'plans from 1800 show a burial ground', but the author was seemingly not aware whether or not the site had been cleared, suggesting there was 'potential for burials to survive'. On both the 1851 Ordnance Survey map and a plan of Wakefield drawn in 1823 by John Walker, a local surveyor, the site was clearly marked 'Unitarian Burial Ground', but on subsequent OS maps, only the site is shown, not the wording.

Hewitt reckoned he'd counted sixty-seven gravestones at the burial ground, an area that he calculated to be between 400 and 500 square feet. He described how he'd accessed the cemetery via a gateway, 'facing the small bridge across the beck.' To his dismay, Hewitt found that the site was being used as a hen yard, and in 1862, during the visit when he copied out the inscriptions, he was noticed by a small boy.

'Pa,' the boy shouted; 'there's someone gone into your hen yard!'

A few weeks later, on a return visit, Hewitt found the hens had been removed, but the site

The site of Westgate End House today. Following arson attacks in 2006 and 2009, the house was torn down, with a solitary, derelict section being all that remained in late 2015.

was full of rubbish, which included 'old leather, the refuse of a shoemaker's workshop; and pieces of tin, the sweepings from a tinner's establishment, in large quantities … and the place appears to have been a receptacle for such and other unseemly deposits.' In spite of all the detritus, he was able, with a bit scrubbing, to make a decent transcription of the writing on the many stones.

The first one he noted read:

Here lieth the Body of Matthew Machan, of Naboth Vineyard, Wakefield, who departed this life the 13th April, 1808, aged 64 years.

Hewitt commented below that he was not aware of a Naboth Vineyard in Wakefield, but acknowledged that 'the Presbyterians made a practice of Christening their children peculiar Scriptural phrases' and duly presumed that Matthew Machan's residence, named after the story from the Old Testament, was similarly inspired. Indeed, on 28 May 1814, the *Leeds Mercury* reported the recent death of 66-year-old Mrs Machan, 'of this town, relict of Mr Machan, late of Naboth Vineyard, Wakefield'.

In Baines's 1822 Yorkshire trade directory, Naboth's Vineyard was occupied by a millwright named Joseph Blackburn.

Another notice, this time appearing in the *Leeds Times* on 27 July 1839, reported the death of Sarah Bell, wife of Mr Benjamin Bell (of Leeds) and 'daughter of the late Mr Matthew Machan, of Naboth's Vineyard, Wakefield. Sarah had been baptised at the chapel on Westgate End on 13 July 1782, aged five weeks and a day old, the entry of her baptism recording that her father, 'Matthew Machin', lived on Kirkgate, with her siblings' baptisms recording Kirkgate or Wrengate as the site of the family home.

A correspondent in the *Bradford Observer* of 4 April 1867 wrote a letter titled 'Kipping Chapel Worthies'. Kipping Chapel is an Independent Chapel in Thornton, near Bradford, and one of its former ministers was Samuel Hulme, who was pastor for forty-six years, and also father of eleven children. Two of his daughters lived at Wakefield, and both were buried at the site. According to the correspondent, their gravestones read as follows:

Under this Tomb are deposited the Remains of Elizabeth Hulme, fourth Daughter, and tenth Child, of the Reverend Samuel Hulme, late Minister at Kippin, in Thornton, near Bradford, in Yorkshire. She departed this life the 13th January, 1769, in the Flower of her Age.

Several lines of verse followed, which included the following:

> *She spake no ill: She thought no wrong:*
> *She liv'd without An Enemy; and died without a Fear:*
>
> *Go gentle Readers, and learn to do the same;*
> *For know that true Riches are in a good name;*
> *No stranger to her Merit, inscrib'd her praise,*
> *But one who knew her from her earliest days*

The reverend's other daughter was called Hannah, and she'd married Stephen Holdsworth, of Wakefield (at Bradford). Hannah had died aged eighty-five, having spent eighteen years as Stephen's wife, and forty-two as his widow. The headstone declared that she had 'worthily' maintained her 'long life' through the 'character of a good Christian'.

As for Stephen, he'd died on 27 September 1763, and his inscription revealed that the couple had been hit by repeated tragedies: he shared a grave with 'five Children, who died in their Infance'.

Also among the buried was Mrs Sarah Aldred, 'Daughter of the Rev J. Aldred, many years Minister of the Protestant Dissenting Chapel, in Westgate, Wakefield. She died 15 February 1832, aged 90 years.'

John Aldred was the minister at the time of Archbishop Herring's visitation, though, of course, the archbishop was concerned with Anglican places of worship, with a passing interest in non-conformist congregations. Aldred was succeeded in his ministry in 1761 by William Turner. In

Old Presbyterian Burial Ground, by Henry Clarke. *By courtesy of WLSL.*

the second volume of *Lives of Eminent Unitarians*, published in 1843 and written by Reverend William Turner junior, the author discussed Turner's succession and described the congregation at Wakefield as 'far from being the most numerous, yet, from the wealth and influence of several of its leading families, was at that time perhaps the most considerable in the north of England.'

Readers of Hewitt might have felt a sense of eerie unease upon learning that there was an abandoned graveyard on their doorsteps, but this would have been nothing compared to the terror experienced by those running for their lives, pursued by a chain-clanking boggart, who chased them up and down what is now Batley Road. Rumours had been spread long ago that this boggart had taken up residence at Alverthorpe Hall, home at the time to Reverend Benjamin Forster, the prolific letter writer. The 'Boggard of Langar Hede', as he was called, was described in one of the Reverend's letters to Gough, the antiquary, dated 2 December 1766. Reverend Forster told Gough that the creature, a padfoot, was of 'old fame'. Langar Hede was a corruption of Longerhead Lane, which Walker confirmed as the name of a road between Balne Bridge and Alverthorpe (which in Forster's day was pronounced Ollerthorpe). A reference to Longerhead Lane appeared in an advert in the *Yorkshire Post and Leeds Intelligencer* on 21 September 1869, when 'valuable manufacturing premises and building land' was offered for sale by auction by the Yorkshire Fibre Company Limited, Bradford Mill, Balne Lane, Wakefield. Lot six of the offering was described as a 'plot of BUILDING LAND, fronting Victoria Street on the east, Lot 1 on the west, Longerhead

The former Warburtons site in 2015.

Lane on the north, on the south by property of Mr Smith, and contains an area of 1,025 square yards'.

The boggart lived in one of the draw wells in the expansive grounds of the Alverthorpe Hall estate and terrified the life out of the servants. Forster described it thus:

[It] … clanks its chain at a three lane end, and so parades it for a few hundred yards up the lane, under a long garden wall belonging to this house. It begins its stalk from a spot where [there] is an old well (one of the three Robin Hood's wells in this Riding) under the present causeway.

There were several witnesses to the boggart's reign of terror, including one man who'd told Reverend Forster that one fateful night he'd walked with the beast a quarter of a mile up the lane described, only to discover, later that same evening, that his beloved aunt had crossed over to the next life. Through this testimony, Reverend Forster was able to supply Gough with a vivid description of the old padfoot:

It is white, with glaring eyes, four-legged (like all our goblins), and about the size of a cawf [calf], and is the most dreaded of all padfoots of this part.

A young lad in Reverend Forster's employ was so scared of encountering the boggart that he wouldn't dare venture to the Reverend's apartment alone, overlooking, as it did, the garden wall that the creature stalked. On the occasions when he felt brave enough to visit the reverend, the boy would insist that he be allowed to take one of the estate's snarling mastiffs with him.

The Reverend also told Gough about a female servant who'd had a close encounter with the boggart. She was so shaken that she handed back her 'godspenny' (a coin given to servants when they were hired by new employers), refusing to work at hall a minute longer, adding: 'Not even if you gave me the house and estate!'

Reverend Forster concluded this passage of his letter with an earnest plea for his friend, Gough, to 'come and help me to exorcise this fierce fiend.'

Long after Forster departed, the hall eventually came into the hands of Joseph Armitage, who died in 1803. His sons, William and Henry, were involved in a tragic accident in August 1809, following a day's game shooting on the moors at Scarborough. Triumphant at their successes at the sport, the pair, riding home in their gig, attempted to cross a brook, swollen by excessive rain. On realizing they weren't going to make it, Henry jumped out and was carried off down the stream to his death, his body discovered the following day. William managed to stay in the gig and his horse was able to convey him to safety, at which point he too jumped from the gig. He was saved, but the horse was not so lucky, and like Henry, was carried away by the water.

By now, Benjamin Clarkson, a local attorney, was owner of the hall. He died in 1820, and after this, the hall was let to tenants, including one George Laurence, a local schoolmaster, who, from 1855, turned Alverthorpe Hall into a private school for young gentlemen. Prior to being declared bankrupt in 1857, Laurence advertised the establishment unsparingly in provincial newspapers. A typical example appeared in the *Huddersfield Chronicle* on 25 July 1857:

THE COLLEGE, Alverthorpe-hall, near Wakefield, for YOUNG GENTLEMEN.
Mr G. LAURENCE, Principal;
Assisted by
The Rev W.E. LITTLEWOOD, B.A., Wrangler, 1854,
Chancellor's Medallist, 1851;
The Rev W.R. BOWDITCH, M.A., Cantab;
And a competent staff of Masters for English, Commercial Subjects, Drawing, Chemistry, German, French, Mineralogy, Geology, Music, Gymnastics, Deportment and Drilling.
    The students are arranged in three departments:-
    1st – The Preparatory or Junior Department, limited to twelve boys, from six to nine years of age, conducted by a lady from one of the training schools, assisted by the principal and the other masters.
    2nd – The Commercial Department, for pupils destined for commercial life.
    3rd – The Higher Department, for youths intended for the universities, the professions, military and civil service, and mining and manufacturing pursuits.

The junior pupils have a separate class-room, playground and lodging-room. All the young gentlemen attend the lectures on chemistry twice-weekly.

Separate beds for each pupil. – All applications to be made to the principal.

The *Huddersfield Chronicle*, on 4 July that same year, reported from 'the College' on the day prizes were distributed to the pupils. The paper suggested that 'a more pleasing celebration it has seldom been our lot to witness,' and the article went on to describe how the grounds were filled with umbrageous trees, flowering shrubs and beautiful plants. Furthermore, the journalist was delighted to see that so many members of the 'fairer creation' had turned out to 'witness the triumphs of the youthful competitors.' Prizes were handed out for scripture history, arithmetic and mathematics, general industry, poetry, French and German, natural science, writing, chemistry, drawing, and history and geography. A local solicitor, who, along with his brother, had been taught by Mr Laurence, gave a speech singing the principal's praises. But less than a year later, George Laurence was listed, in the *Leeds Times*, as one of several insolvent debtors whose case was to be heard on Monday, 19 April 1858. He appeared to have been something of a nomad, described as being late of:

Alverthorpe Hall from a print enclosed in a first edition of Henry Clarkson's *Memories of Merry Wakefield*. Beneath the print is an inscription by Clarkson to his relative, Matthew Clarkson of New York, reading: *With the author's kind regards, Alverthorpe Hall, Wakefield, 23 November 1887.* To this the author added his own name and date of birth, '*17th Decr 1801*'. The book was discovered for sale in a rare book store in Connecticut. Purchased in 2014, it now sits on a bookshelf just half a mile from Henry Clarkson's old home.

No. 22 1/2, Castlegate, in the City of York, also of Sandal Magna, near Wakefield, Yorkshire, occasionally residing at East Keswick, near Wetherby, and at Crampton-street, Bradford, both in Yorkshire, in all the last-named places out of employment, in lodgings, theretofore Alverthorpe Hall, near Wakefield aforesaid, schoolmaster and boarding school proprietor, theretofore of Galway-house, Wakefield aforesaid, schoolmaster and boarding school proprietor, theretofore of Chestnut-grove, and formerly of Westgate, both in Wakefield aforesaid, master of the Proprietary School, Wakefield aforesaid, and also receiving boarders for the school.

The case was duly heard at the Insolvent Debtors' Court, and Laurence was discharged.

Henry Clarkson, nephew of Benjamin Clarkson, was the next high profile tenant, and eleven years after taking the tenancy on, he became owner of the hall when the then owner, his cousin, Clara Clarkson, whose diaries were published in 1971, conveyed the property to him, with some sadness on her part. It was from the hall that the octogenarian wrote his book, *Memories of Merry Wakefield*.

One of the earliest records of the hall's existence appears in Banks's *Walks in Yorkshire: Wakefield and its neighbourhood*. In it he recorded that John Maude, of Alverthorpe Hall, died there in 1635.

The back of Alverthorpe Hall.

Flanshaw Junior and Infant School, which stands on the site of Alverthorpe Hall.

Or had he passed away in an earlier version of the hall, situated at a different location? On 4 January 1938, a curious account appeared in the *Yorkshire Post* under the headline 'Old Alverthorpe Hall?' Exciting discoveries had been made during demolition work in 1937 and 1938 at Milner's Court in Alverthorpe, which stood near the entrance to the Sirdar textile merchants. The newspaper described that a 'half-timbered 15th century building laid bare by the demolition of some old cottages' had been found, packed with treasures of yesteryear. An interior brick wall had been taken down, which revealed around 100 feet 'of fine Elizabethan oak panelling'. The report also described the discovery of 'four old fire places in an excellent state, some hand-made bricks, and some of the timber of the old house [which] will be preserved'. One of these 'massive Tudor fire-places' went to Clarke Hall. The demolition firm J.W. Crossland and Sons apparently found a date stone bearing the year 1341, though the newspaper claimed that this had been lost. It was declared, prematurely, as will be shown, that the building dated to at least the fifteenth century, and opinion was divided as to whether this was the site of the mythical Huntsman Inn, or the site of the original Alverthorpe Hall. It was well known that this area once hosted hunts, memorialized by the houses at Huntsman's Fold, a name that survives today, and that a public house once supplied the huntsmen with victuals.

Milner's Court in the early twentieth century.

The antiquarian Henry Charlesworth Haldane holding what was reputed to be Little John's bow.

H.C. Haldane, of the Wakefield Historical Society, told the newspaper that it was his belief that a house of such size (he thought it probably contained twenty-six rooms), was too big for an inn of that period, not standing on a coaching road. Instead, he was convinced that, together with the oak panelling, the fireplaces and the high quality of the construction, it was far more likely that such a building had once housed an impressive gentry family. He felt that it was this building where John Maude died in 1635. John's grandson, Daniel Maude, who was buried at the parish church on 15 November 1710, then built the Alverthorpe Hall where Clarkson resided. It was suggested that the earlier hall perhaps became a farmhouse upon the erection of the new hall, and then perhaps the Huntsman Inn. The demolition firm also found some brewing rooms and confirmed that cellars existed, which they were planning to excavate.

On 21 and 22 February, further news of the discoveries was printed in the *Yorkshire Post*. It was stated that five letters had been found in one of the oak beams, dating from the seventeenth century. And thus Mr Haldane's suggestion that these remains were once home to the Maude family was disproven. The letters showed that it was actually the Batty family who lived in the building from 1605 (a date confirmed in a frieze found in a ceiling).

Walker explained that the date stone mentioned above was recovered, and it was established that it actually read 1541, not 1341. He also described how the whole of the interior woodwork 'was held together by oak pegs, and when uncovered no trace of rot or fungoid growth was found.' Walker said that the building originally comprised twenty-four rooms, so Mr Haldane was close with his suggestion of twenty-six.

The letters were each addressed to 'Cosen Battey' at 'Alerthorpe', and were described in the newspaper report. Francis Pierrepoint was the writer, and John Batty the recipient. Pierrepoint gave instructions that one of the letters, dated 15 May 1648, was to be left for collection at 'the sign of the Black Swan'. There is a public house of this name still standing on Silver Street in Wakefield, the building dating to the early seventeenth century, but there was also a Black Swan Inn on the original site of the Strafford Arms, which was taken down in 1727. The letter read as follows (the transcription below taken from the newspaper, which has standardized the dated spelling):

The Batty family house shown during its demolition in 1937. *By courtesy of YAHS.*

This day received by the post yours of the 12th instant, and heartily thank you for your purpose to be speedily in Mashamshire. You know how necessary expedition is in the business there. Therefore, I need not further to urge it. You mention you are sending us some money by Richard Pollard. I hope he has warranted it … and is able to satisfy in case of Taylor.

If he hath not done the former nor can the latter, then keep the money until you return forth of Mashamshire. Unless you can return it by clothiers or graziers as I formerly desired you, or by a master carrier who is able and will warrant it.

I had this day news from the committee at Nottingham of some late robberies in the Forest of Sherwood, and it is here reported that a Yorkshire carrier was there robbed of a great sum of money which I mention to you in way of caution. I wish you all happiness, and remain your assured friend, Francis Pierrepont.

The newspaper reporter naturally commented on how the 'shadow of Robin Hood' still hung over the forest.

Not far from the old Batty residence, and Clarkson's Alverthorpe Hall, torn down and eventually replaced by Flanshaw Junior and Infant School, stands Silcoates Hall (otherwise Silcoates House, or just plain Silcoates). Overlooking Wrenthorpe Park and Alverthorpe Meadows, Silcoates was home to the Lumb family, where Mrs Anne Lumb kept diaries. In 1884, Charles Milnes Gaskell,

Silver Street, showing the Black Swan, by Henry Clarke. *By courtesy of WLSL.*

of Thornes House, printed these diaries at his own expense. The entries depicted life at the hall from 1755 to 1757. In the introduction, Milnes Gaskell, who estimated that the hall was built between 1740 and 1750, described the building as 'red-brick with two wings and classical bay-windows on either side of the principal entrance'. He went on:

> Where now are smoke and squalor, filth and garbage, pleasant fields and lanes extended, and the view to St John's over the intervening valley must have been one of the most striking in the neighbourhood. From the Lumbs the Hall passed to the Kendalls, and from them to the present owners, by whom it has been made the dwelling-house of the Master of the Congregational School that is added on to it.

This final point was a reference to Yorkshire Dissenters' Grammar School, which opened at Silcoates in 1820. It wasn't a success, however, and within a decade it was replaced by a new

The Black Swan public house today.

outfit known as the Northern Congregational School, which opened in 1831, the *Bradford Observer* of 3 July 1834 noting it had reached its third anniversary amid celebrations the day before. Its purpose was to provide residential education for the sons of non-conformist clergymen. After navigating a bumpy road, which saw several name changes and then the threat of closure when the whole estate was offered for sale in 1870, all seemed well after the school's trustees were able to obtain sufficient funds to purchase the site themselves at a price of £15,000. A new building, housing classrooms and dormitories, was added, opening on 8 October 1873, when a public meeting dealt with the formalities, followed by luncheon and tea. According to the *Sheffield Daily Telegraph*, on 9 October, the festivities were attended by 'friends from near and distant parts of the country', and the building was described as 'continental in character, quadrangular in form, of red brick, and will cost (with the estate) altogether £20,000'.

In 1897 John Arthur Yonge became the new headmaster, replacing Reverend William Field, who'd held the post for two decades. Then, seven years later, in April 1904, disaster struck.

It was the evening of Wednesday, 13 April, during the Easter holidays (the boys and the masters not in residence), when, at about half-past ten, Mrs Gill, the housekeeper, was alarmed by the smell of burning. She interrupted the servants' supper, and on instructing them to leave the back

Silcoates, 'the Library'.

Silcoates as it looked when it reopened in October 1873. *By courtesy of YAHS.*

kitchen, in which they were gathered, and walk out to the yard, one of the girls spotted a light coming from a dormitory window in the middle story of the building. Two male porters, a Mr Smith and a Mr Walker, were alerted, and it was quickly discovered that a fire had broken out, one that would not be easily extinguished, no matter how many buckets of water were thrown at it. The fire was difficult to get to, and there was much pitch pine where it burned, a highly flammable wood. As a result, the fire spread with great rapidity, and before long the whole place was ablaze; all that those gathered on the lawn outside could do was watch on in horror.

The Wakefield Fire Brigade were alerted, but an engine was not sent. This was because the council had passed a resolution, a few years earlier, directing that the brigade should not attend fires outside the city boundary. Consequently, Chief Constable Harris (otherwise known as Captain Harris), of King Street, who was in charge of the fire brigade, could not persuade Alderman Kilner to allow the city's steamer fire engine to attend the blaze at Silcoates. The school, lying just outside the boundary, would have to fend for itself, though Captain Harris did send several of his crew to try to help.

By the time the crew arrived, a crowd had gathered, having been attracted by the illuminated skies. The firemen could not find any water within a quarter of a mile of the school, leaving the establishment, as the *Wakefield Express* put it on 16 April, 'practically at the mercy of the flames'. It was a relief, therefore, that the eighty schoolboys, who were mostly the sons of congregational ministers from around the kingdom, were not in attendance. The newspaper pointed out that while

Silcoates on fire on 13 April 1904. The headmaster's house is shown on the right.

the boys were away for Easter, 'the premises have for the last few days been in the hands of the painters and decorators.'

Messengers had been dispatched to the home of Mr Thomas Perkin Robinson, of Pinderfields House, the Honorary Secretary and Treasurer of the school. Mr Robinson was also the proprietor of the *Wakefield Express*, having succeeded his father as owner. It was hoped that Mr Robinson would give authority for the Leeds and Dewsbury fire brigades to be summoned. But Captain Harris pointed out that any such attempts would be pointless because there would not be sufficient water to power the steam pumps of either Leeds' or Dewsbury's engines. At this point, Mr Robinson got in his car and drove as speedily as he could to Silcoates, a distance of 2 miles from his house. He arrived about midnight and discovered the true extent of the catastrophe (the buildings being 'completely doomed', according to his paper). A local firm, Messrs Colbeck, tried to help by sending a long hose to the school, but when water was pumped into it, it was discovered that the water pressure from the mains was so low that the flow only went about a foot into the air.

Once again, the idea of sending for help from a nearby brigade was mooted, for it had become apparent that the headmaster's house might be saved if prompt action was taken. This was the original Silcoates House, and shortly before one o'clock in the morning, the fire still raging, a volunteer carried a message by bicycle. He rode as heartily as his lungs would allow, whizzing down the hill upon which Silcoates sits, and then up Bradford Road, on to Bell Street, passing the junction with Balne Lane, close to where the famed Cliff Tree once stood, before eventually arriving at the city police station. From there a telephone call was made and the Dewsbury brigade duly answered, sending three horses and their own steamer, which reached Silcoates at two o'clock. Unfortunately, the firemen did not bring enough hose to reach the distant – and only – supply of water, which Mr Robinson thought might be beneficial in controlling the fire, so it was back to buckets once more.

Despite all hands doing what they could, the cause was deemed hopeless, and some of the furniture belonging to Mr Yonge, the headmaster (who was in Switzerland at the time), was salvaged. When the flames eventually receded, it was clear that the original house had indeed been saved, though the other buildings, and all their contents, were practically destroyed, with the cost of the damage estimated at about £12,000.

It was thought that the origin of the fire was 'due to a flue from the back kitchen which passed through the apartments where the outbreak was first seen.' It was also known that the boiler was defective.

There was considerable fallout in the aftermath of the fire, fingers being pointed in all directions during the days and weeks that followed. The *Leeds Mercury*, reporting on 21 April 1904, from the annual meeting of the Yorkshire Congregational Union, stated that regret was expressed when it was discovered that the school was not adequately insured. Six days later, the newspaper told its readers that Wakefield's Town Clerk, Mr Hudson, had resigned following the debacle over the fire engine, after a resolution asking for him to surrender his post was narrowly passed.

In May, the same paper carried a story referring to the presentation of a report, by the new town clerk at Wakefield. This report revealed that the corporation had previously requested payment of a stipend of £350 per year for the brigade to attend out of town fires, and because this had not been paid, the engine had to stay where it was. An offer had been made by the corporation whereby the rural council could pay this fee over fifteen years, but as Stanley Urban Council had refused, the deal fell through.

At a meeting held in April, Alderman Kilner explained why he had refused the order to send the fire engine to the school, stating that the responsibility of doing so was too great for his shoulders. He duly blamed the rural council.

But what of the school's future? The *Sheffield Daily Telegraph*, reporting on 13 June 1904, explained:

The recent fire by which Silcoates, the well-known Congregational School at Wakefield, was destroyed will be well remembered. It was quickly stated, with some show of authority, that the building would not be rebuilt, and that Silcoates would cease to exist, but it appears that such statements have been too hastily made. At all events, from a circular which summons the members of Silcoates Old Boys' Association together on the 25th inst., it seems that by that date some definite conclusion will have been arrived at with regard to the future of the school. Arrangements have been made whereby a portion of the scholars can be accommodated at Harrogate, and here their work is being done, but we may be permitted to express hope that a new school may be erected on the site of that which has been burned down, and that Silcoates, whose associations are so bright, and with which the early days of so many well-known men are identified, may not be permitted to lapse as a scholastic institution.

At that time, alumni included Sir George Newnes, publisher of *The Strand Magazine* and *Country Life*; Edwin Lawrence Godkin, editor-in-chief of the *New York Evening Post*; and Theodore Cooke Taylor, a Liberal Member of Parliament and businessman, the former two being sons of congregational ministers.

On 9 July, the *Yorkshire Post* told its readers about the fate that had been decided for the school, stating that 'until new premises are erected', Silcoates would be transferred to Saltburn-by-the-Sea in the North Riding of Yorkshire. Here seventy students and five resident masters would be accommodated in a 'handsome block of buildings to the west of the town, formerly known as the Convalescent Home, which commands a fine view of land and sea'. The school would open the following September.

A year later, the *Yorkshire Post* brought news from Saltburn, when it declared that the school had 'more than survived the disastrous fire'. At a meeting of the school's annual subscribers held in Leeds, the chairman, Reverend Bryan Dale, of Bradford, discussed a movement that had been formed with the view to 'building a new school so as to accommodate a much larger number of scholars.'

These plans were given the go-ahead, and on Saturday, 2 November 1907, the foundation stones of the new school were laid at the site of the former establishment. Several Silcoates 'old boys' came to watch, one last chance for them to see the ruins of the familiar buildings destroyed by the fire, before they were pulled down. Newspapers announced that the new school would accommodate 130 boys, nearly doubling the previous numbers.

By February 1908 the building of the new school was well under way. Arnold Hargrave, the plumber whose uncles ran the drapers' shop on Kirkgate, had returned to the trade in 1907, aged seventeen. This followed a stint at sea as a cook, having trained in the plumbing trade at J. Woodhead's, on Charlotte Street, a year earlier. On 28 December 1908, he entered in his diary that he had spent a month aboard SS *Goole* but preferred a life on dry land, writing:

> I left this ship just a month afterwards when I came home to Wakefield and rejoined the plumbing trade. In the second week in Feb 1908 I was sent to a new school under erection just outside Wakefield known as Silcoates School and we finished there in the third week in Nov 1908.

Arnold may have witnessed a terrible accident on 7 September 1908, which occurred during the building of the new school. A local painter, aged thirty, who lived at Bowman Street in Sandal, was busy painting beams inside the new building. He lost his balance and came tumbling from the scaffold he was working on, falling a distance of 12 feet. Unconscious and with a fractured skull, he was taken to Clayton Hospital to recover.

With work finally complete, the new Silcoates Congregational School was opened on 1 October 1908 by Walter Runciman, the Minister for Education, who was presented with a bouquet of red and pink roses by Miss Yonge, daughter of Mr Yonge, who was still headmaster. Mr Runciman formally opened the doors to the school with a specially gilded silver key. The *Yorkshire Post* described the new building:

> The new structure is of brick, with stone facings, and stands three storeys high, with two wings. It contains a large assembly hall, with two class-rooms adjoining, provided with moveable partitions. Immediately behind the assembly hall is a dining hall to seat 120. There are four class-rooms, reading-room, and library, cloak-room, changing room, chemical and physical laboratories, lecture room, and music room. The dormitories will accommodate a hundred boys and staff. The building is in line with and resembles the Georgian architecture of the head master's house, which escaped the flames.
>
> The total cost of the new buildings, including repairs to the head master's house, laying out the front, enlarging and fencing in the playground, and fitting up the chemical laboratory, will be £11,850.

Not all those with a connection to the school were able to celebrate when it reopened. On 4 February 1909, bankruptcy proceedings began against William John Grassby, a farmer based near Silcoates. He was examined at Wakefield Bankruptcy Court where it was determined that his liabilities stood at £397, with a deficiency of £141. He told the court that his failure was down to the loss of a

A postcard showing Silcoates after it had been rebuilt following the fire.

A modern view of the headmaster's house. *By courtesy of Silcoates School.*

The Cliff Tree, by Reverend Kilby, drawn shortly before its demise.

contract to supply milk to the school before it burned down. He said he had been 'pinched' ever since and as a result had resorted to moneylenders who had charged him interest at a rate of 50 per cent. It seems he did not regain the contract.

Silcoates continues to this day as an independent school, operating from its original home between Alverthorpe and Wrenthorpe, with 665 pupils on the register. The school badge incorporates a phoenix, and the establishment's Latin motto, *Clarior ex Ignibus* (brighter out of the flames), ensures the events of April 1904 will not be forgotten.

North of Westgate, close to the new library and museum at Wakefield One, once stood a great wych elm tree, much revered by the inhabitants of the town. Tradition held that it had been planted by John Maude, of Alverthorpe Hall. He was referred to as 'John Maude the elder' in his will, and according to a Maude family legend, he planted the tree in about 1585, some fifty years before his death. According to one of Maude's descendants, the tradition also held that whilst ever the family flourished at Wakefield, so did the tree, but as it began to decay, so did their fortunes.

It was known as the Cliff Tree, or Cliff Hill Tree, and it stood at the top of Balne Lane close to Cliff Field Terrace (now Sandy Walk), where there was formerly a Cliff Field Cottage and where there still remains Cliff Hill House, built in 1840. Today, Wakefield also has Cliff School, Cliff Park

Avenue, Cliff Lane, Cliff Parade, and until fairly recently, the Cliff Tree Inn, which was located on Balne Lane. These names are references to the dramatic topography upon which this part of Wakefield is built, where a sandstone bluff slopes suddenly on its westerly edge, forming a cliff.

In his will, proved at York on 19 April 1635, John Maude left a house with outbuildings and land called the Cliff in Westgate, describing it as:

> That capitall messuage & burgage or Tenement with the Appurtenances wherein I now dwell commonly called and knowen by the name of the Cliff situate lyinge and being in Westgate in Wakefeild aforesaid …

Walker said that a Dr Cookson bought and pulled down a timber-built, plaster-panelled dwelling named Cliff House in 1747, which stood on the north side of Westgate. And it was in the Cliff Field that the building of the new St John's Church was begun in November 1791, the *Stamford Mercury* reporting on 11 November that Reverend Henry Zouch, of Sandal Magna, had 'laid the first stone of a new church at Wakefield.'

John Lee, a Wakefield attorney at law and entrepreneur, so pivotal in the building of the church, had, that September, laid the foundation stone of the new housing development that would become known as St John's Street (later St John's North), before adding St John's Place (now St John's Square). These locations, with their fine Georgian terraced houses, still standing today, were recently used to magically transform Wakefield into London for the BBC drama, *Jonathan Strange and Mr Norrell*.

The new church, dedicated to St John the Baptist, was consecrated by the Archbishop of York, William Markham, on 28 July 1795, during what was described at the time as a 'gala week' for Wakefield. A day earlier, the *Leeds Intelligencer* reported that as well as consecrating the church, the Archbishop planned to confirm thousands of people in the original 'old church' of All Saints, and then on Wednesday the town's 'Grand Musical Festival' would begin in the new church at St John's.

Those 'who are lovers of sweet sounds may expect such gratification as the country seldom affords,' enthused the paper. An advert in the same publication warned would-be attendees that the festival was a ticket only affair, at a cost of £1 1s. to attend the whole event, with no 'trouble or expense spared in procuring a full and select chorus.' Individual performances, which included Handel's *Messiah*, could be enjoyed from as little as 3s. 6d.

Reporting at the conclusion of the gala week, the paper reckoned that the Archbishop had confirmed 5,000 people at Wakefield, followed by 3,000 at Barnsley and another 5,000 at Sheffield. There was also a review of the music festival, which read as follows:

> The Musical Festival at Wakefield last week, was very fashionably although not very numerously attended; the different concerts, selections, &c. were executed with great taste and judgement, and the choruses were full and harmonious. The organ in the above church is pronounced by the *amateurs*, to be a peculiarly fine-toned instrument.

St John's Church in the Cliff Field. *By courtesy of YAHS.*

St John's Church today.

Events that took place earlier in the eighteenth century connected the Cliff Tree and Field Marshal Wade's troops. Wade was Commander-in-Chief of the Forces in 1745, during the Jacobite rising of that year when rebels, led by Charles Edward Stuart, had begun their march to the capital. Word had reached Wade that the Bonnie Prince, who had led his rebels as far as Derby, reaching that town on 4 December, had changed his mind and turned back. He was now heading north in order to make a swift return to Scotland, retreating from the British, who had recalled their troops from the Continent, where they'd been fighting.

That December, newspapers reported that a letter had been received at Whitehall from Field Marshall Wade, sent on the 11th of that month from Wakefield, where his troops had spent the nights of 10th and 11th camping. The letter revealed that a Council of War had taken place at nearby Ferrybridge on 8 December, where it was resolved that:

> the Army should march by the Way of Wakefield and Halifax into Lancashire, in order to intercept the Return of the Rebels Northward; but upon their arrival at the first mention'd Place upon the 10th at Night, Advice having been received that the main Body of the Rebels was then at Manchester, and their advanced Guard gone towards Wigan, on their Way to Preston, by which they had got three or four Days March of the Army under the Marshal, it was resolved to send a Detachment of Calvary under the Command of Major General Oglethorp, to pursue them with all possible Expedition, and that the rest of the Army should march towards, Newcastle, and both the Army and the Detachment of Cavalry, were to march upon the 11th.

Walker, in his history of Wakefield, and Reverend Kilby, in his *Scenery in the Vicinity of Wakefield* (1843), tell the story of how Field Marshall Wade ordered his troops to cut down any trees they encountered. Walker said the order was given so that wood could be used for campfires, whilst Kilby suggested their removal was to allow waggons and ammunition to be transported unobstructed. Either way, this meant the Cliff Tree had to go. Such a miserable end for this ancient tree would have horrified the inhabitants of the town, and it was Wakefield's Captain Burton, the officer who'd put down the riot of 1740, who persuaded Wade to leave this tree to nature. In the end, the Field Marshall was so accommodating that he even ordered a guard to be placed around the tree, and his troops duly camped under it in the cold winter air.

The departing troops, having left Wakefield to head to Newcastle, finally caught up with the Bonnie Prince's rebels, decimating them in battle on 16 April 1746 at Culloden.

It was twenty-one years later when Gough, the antiquary, received another letter from Reverend Forster, of Alverthorpe Hall, commenting on the tree:

> Cliffield tree is an ancient *elm* (if I mistake not) standing over a steep descent just without the town, and commanding a pleasant prospect of a rich, well-inclosed, not ill-wooded valley, bounded with high grounds all round, and the tops of Shuter Nab and other of the Western mountains just visible. Since I came an order has been nailed on it from the Steward of the Duke of Leeds, Lord

of the Manor of Wakefield, forbidding the scandalous undermining of it for gravel, sand, stones, &c.

An advert appeared in the *Leeds Intelligencer* on 15 July 1788, offering for let an impressive house owned by Richard Linnecar, a Wakefield wine merchant, who was also a prolific dramatist, a linen draper, a mason, the coroner, and even, for a time, the postmaster. The house came with vaults, a barn and outbuildings, and in addition the lessee would receive 'a Field of Grass Land, near Cliff Tree, and a pew in Wakefield Church'.

In 1838, the Geological Society purchased a plot of land adjacent to the Cliff Tree and in June 1838 it was reported, in the *Leeds Times*, that plans were afoot to erect a 'splendid hall and museum' at the site. And on 25 February 1843, the *Leeds Mercury* reported that 'a table of a gentleman in Wakefield has been supplied with new potatoes from Christmas to the present time, grown in the open air near Cliffe Tree.' According to the paper, rows of the crop were still in place, and 'if properly protected from the frost, they will keep in good condition for a month or two longer.'

John Hewitt elegized about the tree in the same year that Kilby published his *Scenery*, writing the following lines in 1843 in his *Ballad of Cliffe-Hill-Tree, Wakefield*:

> *A Tree there is in Wakefield town*
> *That's noted o'er the world;*
> *And now this Tree is ancient grown,*
> *With cent'ries rounds its whirl'd*
>
> *And num'rous, famous, are its claims,*
> *Which gain it high esteem,*
> *And not the least are children's games,*
> *Which oft around it teem*
>
> *And lovers can repeat with glee*
> *How in their brightest days,*
> *What hours they've spent beneath this Tree,*
> *Tho' wandering near were fays!*
>
> *Its boughs are fading fast away,*
> *Its hast'ning to its end:*
> *'Twould form a theme for Poet's lay –*
> *To future days descend*

He was right to suggest the tree was nearing its end, and somewhat ill-fatedly, in 1845, he penned further verses about the tree, one which went:

Old Cliffe-Hill-Tree has stood the keenest storms,
Of Ages buried now within the Past,
Has laugh'd at what the hurricane performs
Devastating places with destruction's blast

The next news of the Cliff Tree came on 29 November 1845, when the *Leeds Intelligencer,* in a report containing, perhaps somewhat surprisingly, considerably greater detail than its counterpart the *Wakefield Express*, imparted the sad news of its demise:

> The celebrated Cliffe-hill tree which for upwards of two centuries has thrown out its arms in defiance and 'laughed at the storm' has been destroyed. The high wind which prevailed on Wednesday last will long be remembered by the inhabitants of Wakefield, for having robbed them of one of the most interesting objects of that town. Singular as it may appear to many, and foolish as it may seem to some, there was not one person in Wakefield but learnt the intelligence with a sigh, and exclamation of deep heartfelt melancholy. No wonder that such was the case. Independently of its being a splendid natural curiosity it was endeared to hundreds in Wakefield by numberless fond associations which made it to them an interesting object indeed.

Hewitt described the storm as being a most violent one, which blew down several trees, removed chimneys and took the slates off the roofs of local houses. He claimed that when word spread of the fate of the Cliff Tree, thousands of people flocked to the site to see it in its sorry state of destruction. Before long a cabinet was fashioned from its wood by George Dickinson, and this was presented to the first mayor of Wakefield, George William Harrison, who, in four years' time, would have his hat knocked off in the bonfire riots of November 1849. Hewitt explained that the cabinet was later proudly displayed in Mr Loveday's silversmith shop on Silver Street, adding that a 'number of snuff-boxes and other fancy articles were also made from the wood, and were much prized by the holders of them.'

A year and a day after the tree fell, the *Bradford and Wakefield Observer; and Halifax, Huddersfield, and Keighley Reporter* recalled the sad event. It said that George Dickinson, the cabinet maker, had counted the rings of the old tree and concluded that there were in excess of 200, some 'not less than three quarters of an inch in thickness, which indicates it to have had an extraordinary rapid growth at one period of its existence.'

Earlier that year, in August 1846, a curious story concerning George Dickinson and Reverend Sharp, of the parish church, appeared in the *Leeds Times.* It suggested that on the previous Monday night, Dickinson had applied for a summons against Reverend Sharp, alleging that the cleric had assaulted him on 21 August:

> It appears that Mr Sharp disputes the right of road through the church-yard, which has been open
> for centuries; and one fine day, finding the complainant going through the yard with a plank across

his shoulder, attempted to thrust him down the yard steps. The magistrates appeared to think they had no jurisdiction; but on the complainant pressing the case, the summons was granted.

Reverend Sharp duly appeared at the Court House to answer the charge. The court heard that Mr Dickinson had no choice but to take this route, for his house was situated within the churchyard itself. He'd lived there for the past fifteen years, had no other way to reach his door, and his right of access had never been questioned before. Reverend Sharp told the magistrates that he was trying to prevent the desecration of the churchyard, and they had no right to try him on such a charge, but he did acknowledge that Mr Dickinson, and the public in general, did indeed have a right of way, and as such, the Reverend was fined ten shillings and told to think carefully before taking the law into his own hands in future.

Wakefield was in the news again twelve years later, when popular novelist Charles Dickens appeared in the town. It was September 1858, the year he separated from his wife, and he was in the middle of a reading tour, his first of a commercial nature. Wakefield was one of the towns he visited, followed by readings given in Harrogate, York, Leeds and Bradford. An advert promoting the Wakefield reading appeared in the *Wakefield Express* on 4 September, which read:

Mr CHARLES DICKENS WILL READ

At the EXCHANGE BUILDINGS, Wakefield on THURSDAY EVENING, September 9 at Eight o'clock, his

CHRISTMAS CAROL

PLACES FOR THE READING:- Stalls (numbered and reserved), Five Shillings; Area, Half-a-Crown, Gallery and Back Seats, One Shilling

Tickets to be had of Messrs Hicks and Allen, Booksellers, where a Plan of the Stalls may be seen.

The reading will last two hours.

It certainly seemed that the audience were in for a treat. The book had received widespread critical acclaim when it was published fifteen years earlier, and Dickens was a household name by now. And if a review in the *Leeds Intelligencer* on 4 September 1858 of a performance given in Ireland was anything to go by, it seemed the gifted writer was just as adept at narrating his works:

Such clearness and flexibility of voice – such exhaustless mobility of features – such power of eye – such naturalness of gesture (wherever gesture becomes at all requisite, and only there) – and, to crown all, a manner so exquisitely unaffected, and easy, and gracefully familiar! What can one do more than say what has already been said, that Charles Dickens reads his 'Christmas Carol' gloriously. He brought to our ears the mumbling tones of old Scrooge, the shrill squeak of Poor Tiny Tim, and the silvery counter-tenor of that plump sister of Scrooge's niece by marriage, upon whom Topper had cast an eye, and in respect of whom his conduct was so flagrantly suspicious during the game of 'Blind Man's Buff', on that happy Christmas evening. He did this, and everything else which could add point and force and expression to his story, and when he had concluded was greeted with a shower of plaudits.

Odd then, perhaps, that the reading given at Wakefield seemed not to please all those who gathered to hear it. The *Wakefield Express*, reporting on 11 September, thought it needless to review Dickens's performance, because 'the readings of this talented and popular author have been so often and so fully criticized, both in London and provincial papers, that any remarks of ours on that subject are quite unnecessary.' According to the paper, a 'large, and on the whole, select audience' had gathered, but, the report continued, 'we were sorry to observe that some ladies, who, by their position in the very front of the stalls, might naturally be expected to have known better, had the bad taste to leave their seats during the last quarter of an hour's reading, when the general attention would least bear to be disturbed.' The author of the article found it hard to believe 'that any lady could have been guilty of such discourtesy either to the reader or the remainder of the audience,' and thought it quite appropriate that 'some of the assembly express[ed] their disapproval by hissing the fair offenders.'

Westgate audiences had form for this sort of thing. Writing in his 1892 book, *The Old Wakefield Theatre*, author William Senior recalled a notice from this period. It was displayed on a wall at the original theatre, before it was condemned and then demolished in 1894. Shown in the image opposite, this older theatre was situated on the site of the current Theatre Royal, on the junction with Drury Lane. The notice read:

persons entering the Theatre in a state of intoxication, smoking, throwing orange peel, nutshells, &c., shouting, or personally addressing the musicians or other individuals in the Theatre, or in any way disturbing or annoying the audience, will be instantly removed by the constables, who are in constant attendance to preserve order.

Another notice informed patrons that 'season tickets for the Boxes for ten nights' performances can be obtained *if applied for by parties of known respectability.*'

Following his reading at Wakefield, Dickens performed readings of the *Poor Traveller*, *Boots at the Holly Tree Inn* and *Mrs Gamp* at St George's Hall, Bradford on 14 October 1858. An advert announcing the performance, which appeared in the *Bradford Observer* on 23 September, included the following plea (an oblique reference, perhaps, to what had taken place at Wakefield):

On only one occasion, within Mr Dickens's experience, some ladies and gentlemen in the stalls caused great inconvenience and confusion (no doubt unintentionally) by leaving their places during the last quarter of an hour of the Reading, when the general attention could least bear to be disturbed. This elicited a strong disposition in other parts of the Hall towards an angry but not unreasonable protest.

In case any portion of the company should be under the necessity of leaving before the close of the Reading in the apprehension of losing railway trains, they are respectfully entreated, as an act of consideration and courtesy towards the remainder, to avail themselves of the opportunity afforded by the interval between the parts when Mr Dickens retires for five minutes.

The Wakefield venue where Dickens had performed had opened in 1838, replacing an earlier corn exchange, shown below, which stood centrally at the top of Westgate. It had been built by the banker, Thomas Rishworth, and had opened in 1820. But five years later, following the collapse of the bank of Wentworth, Chaloner and Rishworth, in which company Rishworth was junior partner and manager of the Wakefield branch on Westgate, he was ruined and his property claimed by his creditors. Henry Clarkson remembered the day of the bank's collapse, which had its headquarters in London, and well he might have done, as it appears the news sent shockwaves through the town.

News of the company's demise soon reached Leeds. Reports in the local papers there suggested there had been a run on all the banks in Wakefield, beginning on Thursday, 8 December 1825, which had continued over the following days, forcing the banks to open an hour earlier and close an hour later to cope with the demand. The Wakefield correspondent for the *Leeds Intelligencer* sent his paper a worrying report on 14 December:

A great sensation was occasioned in this town and neighbourhood on the evening of Friday Last, by the unexpected tidings that the Banking-house of Messrs Wentworth, Chaloner, and Rishworths had stopped payment. The number of notes issued by this firm, and the general confidence they had hitherto secured, made the shock still greater. On Saturday morning, the neighbourhood of the Bank was crowded with persons flocking in from the immediate district, and throughout the whole of that day, Westgate exhibited the appearance of a fair. The Bank, of course, was open, but the countenances of those who came out, were sufficiently indicative of the result of their enquiries. Several friends of the partners had interviews with them during Friday night and Saturday, and we believe we may state with confidence that, though a temporary inconvenience may arise, there is no doubt that the House will, at no very distant period, discharge to the full all the demands upon it.

The Old Theatre, Wakefield, from William Senior's book of the same name, published in 1894.

The Theatre Royal today, with the Black Horse public house shown on the left.

Despite this optimism (which was misguided, for the firm's bankruptcy would soon be confirmed), the correspondent admitted that 'there must be great distress amongst the lower classes, whose earnings have generally, if not always for the last eight years, been received in the notes of this bank.' He ended his report with a reference to the corn market in Wakefield, stating that 'the importance of Wakefield as a corn market is well known and it is said that the quantity of their [the bank's] paper running, which has been given in payment for consignments of grain from Norfolk, Suffolk, &c. is very large.'

As Wakefield's corn market continued to grow, it was decided, in 1836, that a larger, more suitable venue was required to handle the vast quantities of grain and malt that were being traded in the town. The Wakefield Exchange Building Company was duly formed, and several newspapers reported on the plans. In early March 1836, the *Leeds Mercury* informed its readers that:

we hear that it was decided on Monday, to build a new Exchange at Wakefield. The place fixed upon is that occupied by the row of shops reaching from the top of Market-street to the corner of Queen-street, and extending backwards as far as Mr Barthop's house.

A month later, the *Leeds Times* suggested that a Mr Billington, 'a gentleman who occupies a very respectable station as an architect', had come up with a design that he thought should be incorporated, but he was told that the matter would be decided by a public competition, and that the chosen building would be executed 'on a very extensive and ornamental plan'. The funds to buy the site and finance the construction of the building were raised by issuing shares, 500 of which were offered at £25 each.

On 29 October 1836, the *Leeds Intelligencer* announced that Mr William L. Moffat, of Doncaster, had submitted the winning plan, and on 3 May 1837, the *Leeds Times* described its imminent construction:

NEW CORN EXCHANGE – It is understood that the foundation stone of the New Corn Exchange Buildings, at Wakefield, will be laid on the 24th inst. by the Earl of Mexborough, on which occasion it is expected there will be a Masonic procession, as the Free Masons of the district partake of their annual dinner, in Wakefield, on that day.

The date chosen coincided with Princess Victoria's birthday (she would become queen on 20 June that year), and the day was given as a general holiday in the town. Factories were closed, and shortly after nine in the morning the bells of the parish church rang a 'merry peal', and according to the

The old Corn Exchange, by Henry Clarke. *By courtesy of WLSL.*

Looking up Westgate during the late nineteenth century, showing the old Corn Exchange in the distance. Note the Great Northern Hotel, standing opposite the modern Wakefield Civil Justice Centre. *By Courtesy of YAHS.*

Leeds Times, 'a more than ordinary arrival of carriages and well-dressed pedestrians flocked into the town, thus adding an excitement and interest to an already interesting occasion.' The principal event was, however, not the future queen's birthday, but the laying of the foundation stone of the Corn Exchange.

A public procession, consisting of the whole body of Freemasons, Odd Fellows, &c. with their regalia, of the district, besides public bodies, the shareholders in the undertaking, gentlemen of the town and neighbourhood, bands of music, splendid banners, &c. was formed opposite the Court-House, in Wood-street whence they proceeded to the site of the building. The ceremony of laying the foundation stone was then proceeded with by the Earl of Mexborough, who was presented with a silver trowel … The stone having been lowered to its bed, and the accustomed preliminaries having been gone through, his lordship delivered an address, and the ceremony being concluded, the procession returned by way of Silver-street to the Court-house, where the different bodies separated. At four o'clock the shareholders and their friends partook of a most splendid and sumptuous dinner, at the house of Mrs Bywater, the Great Bull Inn, in Westgate,

The same scene today.

where the evening was afterwards spent with the greatest hilarity; the usual loyal, patriotic, and other toasts, appropriately introduced and responded to, filled up the hours in the most agreeable manner.

There was a sudden interruption in the building work just five days after the foundation stone was laid when the bricklayers downed their tools and 'turned out' at breakfast time because a man had been set on who was not in their union. This matter was obviously resolved to one or both parties' satisfaction, because on 25 November the *Leeds Mercury* reported that 'smart progress' was being made in the undertaking of the building work 'and such portion … as will be devoted to the Corn trade exclusively will, it is expected, be ready in the course of three weeks or a month. Upwards of fifty stalls, at six pounds per annum, have already been taken.'

It was the first Friday of the New Year, 5 January 1838, when the building was partially opened, with a total of forty-six stalls operating; the *Leeds Intelligencer* reporting, on 13 January, that the 'New Corn Exchange at Wakefield was opened yesterday week, for the purposes of the market only. It is well adapted for the purpose, and the accommodation afforded gave great satisfaction.'

Building continued throughout the year, a saloon being erected on the upper floor during the erection of which a local workman fell 30 feet while fixing roof supports. Fortunately, he was found to be less injured than had been feared, and he made a recovery.

In November 1839, it was reported in the same paper that the 'splendid public room' in the Corn Exchange 'was thrown open for the first time' for a special tea to commemorate the anniversary of the Wesleyan Methodist Society. Charity balls, concerts, lectures and course readings were all given in the saloon. The first concert to be hosted at the venue was conducted by Mr White (presumably Edward White, of Hardy Croft, professor of music and organist at the parish church, and son-in-law of the late William Baiston Smith, landlord of the Strafford Arms). The room was described as noble, and the concert received a glowing review in the *Leeds Mercury*, which reckoned 'Mr White conducted the Orchestra in a steady, masterly manner, and has done himself great credit, in giving this charming treat to the lovers of music.' Songs such as *Sweet Bird*, *Batti Batti*, *Stormy Petrel* and *Christmas Holly* were all performed.

Adverts appeared in the local press, promoting further concerts during the years that followed; and in 1847 it cost four shillings for front row seats to listen to songs performed by Mrs Wood, Miss Whitnall and Mr Phillips. The price dropped to two shillings and sixpence if seats at the back were taken, with places in the gallery costing just one shilling and sixpence.

An annual charity ball was held at the building in 1851, and on this occasion the saloon presented a 'brilliant and animated appearance'. The entertainment was 'kept up to a late hour', with a quadrille band providing the music, to which many of the town's illustrious families danced along.

It seems that the Corn Exchange was the preferred venue for most major celebrations taking place in the West Riding at this time. In 1850, the *Leeds Mercury* was busy campaigning for the erection of a public hall in Leeds, spacious enough 'to accommodate large public meetings', and the paper recorded its admiration for Wakefield's Corn Exchange Buildings, 'which are chosen principally because they hold many more persons than any room in Leeds.'

The erection of Wakefield's Corn Exchange had certainly proved timely, for during the railway boom the town's trade in grain and malt was flourishing. Discussing the advent of the railway age, David Joy, in volume eight of the *Regional History of the Railways of Great Britain* series, stated that 15,000 quarters of grain were handled weekly in Wakefield, with the malt market dealing in similar numbers.

Apart from Oakenshaw Station, situated 2 miles away, the first railway station within the town of Wakefield itself was opened at Kirkgate in 1840, and though the building was no more than a little wooden hut (the building that replaced it, which still stands today, was completed in 1857), this new station served the town well, helping to bring more trade to Wakefield.

Even with all the space provided at the Corn Exchange, the ground floor was enlarged in 1864 to accommodate more corn sellers; the original forty-six stalls had grown to seventy-nine, and space for more was desperately required. Following the extension work, the improved building reopened on 24 March of that year, and was described in the *Leeds Intelligencer* two days later as thus:

The Corn Exchange shown in an old postcard.

The Corn Exchange shown in the early twentieth century.

The New Corn Exchange at Wakefield is now so far finished that the factors transacted business in it on Thursday. It is a very handsome and commodious building, nearly double the size of the old Exchange, which was of no mean proportion. Forty-two new stalls have been placed inside, which make up the number at present to 121. The roof of the building is of glass, and affords a very large amount of light, which to both factors and buyers is a *sine qua non*.

A lavish dinner was held to mark the reopening, attended by the directors of the building, as well as buyers, sellers and several invited guests.

Two decades later, the Corn Exchange hosted a 'Graunde Fancie Fayre' promoted by the Wesleyan Methodists in the Wakefield circuit. It was held in October 1887, as part of a drive to raise £2,000 to clear debts owed by the West Parade Chapel, and it was hoped that a grand bazaar and fete at the Corn Exchange would help to realize the debt. One of the attractions was a display of models of old buildings that had stood in Wakefield in bygone days. They were designed by local tailor and active Wesleyan, John William Crosland, who kept a shop on Westgate. Among

The Corn Exchange shown after it was enlarged in 1864.

Exchange House, built on the site of the Corn Exchange.

his models were depictions of Heath Old Hall, Bunny Hall (which had stood at Newton Bar), and the keep of Sandal Castle. Also on display were little half-timber fronted buildings, and models of ancient houses with straw roofs.

According to Walker, the fortunes of the Corn Exchange soon diminished, and its days were numbered. 'As the twentieth century approached,' he wrote, 'the manner of doing business in the corn market changed, and most of the stands became tenantless.' As a result of the corn market's decline, the use of the building changed, and among other things, it became a billiard hall and an auction house, offering cut-price bulk items for sale. Bargain hunters could bid for lots such as thousands of boxes of sweets or biscuits, various types of furniture, quantities of football jerseys, and even hockey sticks. By 1929, the building itself was up for grabs. The notice of sale, which appeared in the *Yorkshire Post* on 20 July, revealed some of the other uses that the old building had been put to:

John William Crosland. *By courtesy of David Smith*

West Parade Wesleyan Chapel. *By courtesy of YAHS.*

PRELIMINARY ANNOUNCEMENT
SALE OF LARGE AND IMPORTANT WAKEFIELD BUILDINGS
Messrs ALBERT HUDSON AND SONS,
of Crown Court, Wood Street, Wakefield have pleasure in announcing that they have been favoured with instructions from the Wakefield Exchange Building Co., Ltd, to offer for Sale by Public Auction, in the early Autumn of 1929.
VALUABLE AND IMPOSING FREEHOLD PROPERTY, known as
THE CORN EXCHANGE, WESTGATE, WAKEFIELD
Comprising BANK AND BUILDING SOCIETY PREMISES, PICTURE HOUSE,
MOTOR GARAGE, SHOPS and OFFICES, etc. situate in the centre of the city.
Further particulars will be contained in future advertisements. Permission to view may be obtained from the Auctioneers, or from CATTERALL, SON and BOULTON, Solicitors, King Street, and Barstow Square, Wakefield.

On 26 October 1929, the same newspaper reported that the building had been sold for £15,800 to Alderman Rowland White at a sale that had attracted 300 people. The building, it was explained, was made of stone 'with three extensive street frontages: possesses two large halls, one now used as a cinema and the other for billiards; and provides office accommodation for a bank and building society and shops for several tradesmen.'

Alderman White, a Wakefield native who held several local offices, including treasurer of Wakefield Conservative Club, chairman of the Wakefield Commercial Travellers' Association, president of the Chocolate and Candy Club, and a member of the Wakefield and District Chamber of Trade Benevolent Institute, became mayor of Wakefield in 1938. That was also the year he opened, with a special silver key, the original swimming baths on Sun Lane, and established a fund to raise money towards the restoration of the Chantry Chapel. Reports stated that Mr White had raised a total of £1,300, and had only been thwarted in his attempts to raise £2,000 by the outbreak of war. As a result of his fundraising, a new frontage was added to the chapel in 1940.

On 20 December 1950, a fire broke out at the Grand Electric Cinema, which was housed in the Corn Exchange. The cinema was known as the 'Ranch' on account of the number of Westerns shown there. A member of staff was alerted by the smell of smoke, soon realizing that beams in the roof were ablaze. It was quickly extinguished and screenings resumed later that day.

As well the cinema, shops and cafés, the building was also used as a roller-skating rink called the Rollerhome. An advert for the rink, placed in the *Leeds Mercury* in April 1939, offered 'roller skating every evening 8 p.m. to 11 p.m.' with admission set at a shilling for participants, or sixpence for spectators. Rink hockey took place on Tuesdays, and the company reckoned theirs was the 'finest skating surface outside London'.

In May 1952, there was another fire. A skater had dropped a cigarette on to the sawdust-covered floor, and not long after the rink had been closed for the evening, the floorboards began smouldering. Firemen discovered the cigarette end and no real damage was done.

The restoration of 'the Chapel on the Bridge' shows that work was underway in 1939. *By courtesy of YAHS.*

Following a further fire in the early 1960s, the decision was taken to tear the grand old building to the ground, and it was duly demolished in July and August 1963. It was soon replaced by Exchange House, which still stands to date, currently housing a sports equipment shop, having opened as a branch of C&A before being taken over by Argos. A blue plaque is the only reminder that a thriving corn market once stood on this site.

A recently erected building on Burton Street, just off Westgate, is the museum within Wakefield One. It is home to the shaft of a cross that is believed to have once stood in All Saints' churchyard, and then subsequently, perhaps, in the old market place within the Bull Ring. It dates to Saxon times, and has lately been on loan to Wakefield from its current owners, the Yorkshire Museum in York, situated on the site of the ruined St Mary's Abbey.

Legend suggests that the shaft was discovered in 1861 by Edmund Waterton of Walton Hall, son of the famous naturalist and explorer, Charles Waterton. Edmund was a Fellow of the Society of Antiquaries, and a keen collector of rare pieces, notably posie rings. Walker suggested that

The restored frontage of the Chantry Chapel shown in 1940. *By courtesy of YAHS.*

Mr Waterton was visiting a butcher's shop on Westgate when he made the rare find. In his book about Wakefield, Walker stated that 'on the demolition of the shop in the following year, [Waterton] obtained the portion of the cross remaining and set it up at the junction of two roads in the wood at Walton.'

In April 1870, following financial difficulties, Edmund Waterton was declared bankrupt, and his collections were broken up. Later that year, the shaft was sold to the Yorkshire Philosophical Society. At their monthly meeting on 1 November 1870, which was held at the Yorkshire Museum, a statement was given concerning the society's recent acquisition of the piece. At the time, it was on display in the lower room of the Hospitium within the remains of the abbey. The statement, reprinted in the *York Herald* on Saturday, 5 November 1870, was written by Reverend Canon Raine, the museum's honorary curator of antiquities, but delivered in his absence by Reverend Kendrick. It reveals the true story of the shaft's discovery, which was actually made by a local man named Mr Harrison.

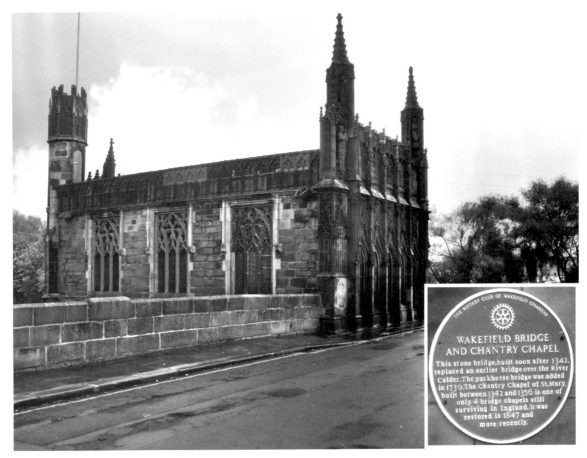

The Chantry Chapel today.

The cross in question was found some years ago in Wakefield, by Mr Harrison, constituting the doorstep to a barber's shop. Mr Harrison gave it to Mr Edmund Waterton, who showed it to me in an outhouse at Walton. It was his intention to set it up in a mortuary chapel, which he proposed to erect over the remains of his father, the well-known naturalist. Mr E. Waterton's collections were dispersed, as you know, in the course of the summer, and thinking that this cross might be lost among the many fragments of wood and stone by which it was surrounded, my wish was to secure it for our Museum, if it could be purchased for a reasonable sum. At my request Mr Fairless Barber went over to Walton to look after the stone, and through his kind agency it was offered to this Museum by Canon Browne (on the part of Mr Waterton), and Mr Harrison (its discoverer), on the condition of our taking care of it. The thanks of the society are due therefore to those gentlemen, but especially to Mr Barber, who took very much trouble in securing the stone for us. The stone itself is 5 feet in length, and three of its sides are sculptured with that interlacing work, which was so common from the 7th to the 10th century. If it has ever borne an inscription, it has been on the side which the friction of thousands of feet has rendered pain. You will remember that at Dewsbury there are some interesting fragments of Saxon sculpture. This is the only piece as yet discovered at Wakefield. It is by far the finest specimen of Saxon art that the Museum at York possesses.

Reverend Kendrick added that 'the best thanks of this meeting be presented to Edmund Waterton Esq., for the gift of a sculptured Saxon cross, and to Fairless Barber, Esq., the Rev Canon Raine, the Rev Canon Browne, and Mr Harrison, of Wakefield for their kind offices in procuring for the society this valuable relic of Saxon art.'

It's clear from the statement (and Reverend Kendrick's subsequent motion) that the idea of Edmund Waterton discovering the shaft while out shopping on Westgate is ludicrous, and that it was this Mr Harrison, presumably connected to the shop where it served as a doorstep, who simply alerted Mr Waterton to its existence.

The shop apparently stood on or close to the site of the present Unity Hall, though Reverend Raine's statement suggested the shop in question was a barber's, whilst Walker asserted it was a butcher's shop.

The original location of the cross is unclear, with some writers suggesting it stood in the churchyard, others insisting it was in the market place, though there was a theory that its home was on or by the bridge at Kirkgate. It's perhaps more likely there were three crosses, one existing at each site.

Whilst discussing the Saxon cross in *Wakefield its History and People*, Walker drew attention to the will of Anne Rawson, which was written on 24 March 1545/6. Anne was a 'Waikefelde' gentlewoman who recorded in the will her wish to be buried 'in the church yerde of Alhalloes of Waikefelde before the crosse'. This is the latest reference that Walker had discovered pertaining to the cross, and he went on to say that there was no record of when it was removed, though he suspected this happened during the sixteenth century, or in consequence of the capture of Wakefield in 1643, when Roundheads 'pulled down the cross in the market place.'

Saxon cross shaft. *By courtesy of Wakefield Council, object on loan from York Museums Trust (Yorkshire Museum).*

Walker went on to refer to a high cross that had stood at the bottom of Kirkgate as far back as 1420. He knew about this cross because he'd read the will of one Joan de Thorp, the widow of a Wakefield mercer. She made her will on 12 April 1420, and it was proved on 26 November that same year. In the document, held today in the archives of the Borthwick Institute at York, the testator, writing in Latin, bequeathed three shillings and four pence in order to make repairs (*ad repairem make*) to the road between (*via inter*) the bridge (*ponte*) and the high cross (*& alta crux*) at the bottom, or end, of Kirkgate (*ad fine Kirkgait*).

As stated earlier, the antiquary, John Leland, had also noted a cross in this location when describing the death of the Earl of Rutland during the Battle of Wakefield in 1460: 'at this place is set up a Crosse *in rei memoriam.*' And in citing an additional manuscript in the collection of the British Library (Add. MSS. 24,470), Walker included a passage written by Dr Johnston, of Pontefract, a contemporary and associate of Ralph Thoresby, of Leeds, the seventeenth- and eighteenth-century diarist and antiquarian. Dr Johnston thought, like Leland, that this cross by the bridge was erected after the 1460 battle, leading Walker to wonder whether they were both mistaken. Walker suggested that the cross referred to was actually the one that was standing in Joan de Thorp's day, presumably having been removed for repairs in the forty years between her will and the battle.

Dr Johnston said of the 'memorial' cross: 'it was taken away about twenty-five years ago, and set up in the Monday Market-place, but then pulled down and defaced in the wars. The pedestal stands yet there.' He was, of course, referring to the Civil War, and specifically the siege at Wakefield in 1643.

The defaced cross, Walker explained, had survived the molestations of the Roundheads, 'for in 1684, forty-one years after the second battle of Wakefield, Ann Smith was ordered to stand upon Wakefield market cross for selling ale on Sunday in the time of Divine Service.'

Of course, as has been described in the chapter about Northgate, a new market cross was erected at the beginning of the eighteenth century, when the inhabitants of Wakefield raised by subscription the necessary means to erect a suitable place to sell their dairy produce.

So, in 1420, a high cross stood at the end of Kirkgate; in 1545, Anne Rawson wished to be buried before a cross in the churchyard (which certainly stands at one end of Kirkgate); in 1643, a cross was defaced in the market place; and in 1684, Ann Smith was made to stand upon 'Wakefield market cross'.

Whatever the locational history of Wakefield's Saxon cross, erected as a signpost to some early place of worship, or perhaps to designate the site of an ancient market, or indeed whether or not the above accounts describe several crosses or just one, the preservation of the shaft of the Saxon cross has allowed the modern visitor a chance to view and touch a Wakefield relic dating back well over 1,000 years.

In May 1933, a replica of the shaft was unveiled at Wakefield Cathedral. It was handed over to the then provost, Noel Hopkins, by J.W. Walker himself, who had campaigned for the return of the original from York. The story made the news, and the *Yorkshire Post* printed an article in its 11 May edition.

For some years [Walker] had been in correspondence with the museum authorities … trying to get the stone back to Wakefield, but he had failed altogether.

The Wakefield Historical Society, who desired some token of early Christianity in the Cathedral Church, decided to subscribe the cost of having the replica made.

The Bishop said the replica, placed near the monument to the first Bishop of Wakefield [Walsham How], linked the new See of Wakefield with the original Christian life of the place.

Alluding to the scaffolding which is at present erected in the nave of the Cathedral, his Lordship said the main beams were unsafe because of the depredations of the death watch beetle, but the building was now quite secure for worshippers.

Members of the Historical Society were conducted round the Cathedral by Mr Walker, and later, after taking tea as guests of Mrs Sowray Greaves at Thornhill House, they proceeded to the Chantry on the Bridge, and to Sandal Castle, under presidential guidance.

The 1933 replica has recently been on display within the chapel at the former Wood Street Police Station, and it was confirmed in 2015 that as part of the restoration project at Wakefield Cathedral, a new, 10-foot high stone cross would be carved in the Saxon style by artist and lay canon, Celia Kilner, and housed outside the West door of the old parish church of All Saints, Wakefield Cathedral since 1888.

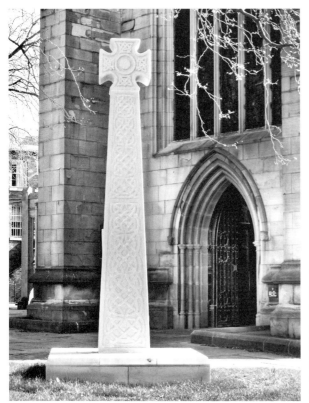

The newly erected replica of Wakefield's Saxon cross, which stands at the west door of Wakefield Cathedral. As only the shaft of the original cross survives, Celia Kilner has based her design on the illustration used in Walker's history of Wakefield, drawn by Walker's wife, Ethel. The cathedral's current logo incorporates the top of Walker's imagined cross.

Index